CLIL
Business Management

Ikuko Ueno Tae Funakoshi Brandon Kramer

chief editor : Shigeru Sasajima

SANSHUSHA

はじめに

　本教科書は、Business management（ビジネス経営）の初歩を英語で学ぶことを想定しています。英語を使ってビジネスの世界で活躍したい人にとっては、最初の一歩として大いに役に立つテキストに構成してあります。

　CLIL（Content and Language Integrated Learning: 内容と言語を統合した学習）では、内容（Content）、思考（Cognition）、コミュニケーション（Communication）、文化間理解（Culture）という「4つのC」（4Cs）を考慮して学ぶことを大切にしています。本教科書は、専門領域の英文から、グローバル化が進む現代のビジネスについて、知識と英語表現の両方を身につけることを目標としています。CLIL学習の特徴である、統合学習（Integrated learning）を活かして、ビジネス経営の基礎と英語をいっしょに学ぼうということです。

　Business management の分野では英語は必須と言ってもよいでしょう。しかし、ビジネスの世界は、英語だけではなく日本語やその他の外国語も必要です。さらには、政治、社会、文化など多様な知識も重要で、すべてを総合して思考することが、おもしろく、やりがいのある（fulfilling and rewarding）仕事に繋がります。それはCLILとよく似ています。

　授業では、Business management という内容（Content）を、主体的に理解し、考えながら学び（Cognition）、英語を「聞き、読み、話し、書く」という対話的な活動を通じて、英語をコミュニケーションの道具として使い（Communication）、多様な多文化社会において適切に判断できる（Culture: Intercultural awareness）活動が期待されます。CLILの理念とBusiness management はとても相性がよいのです。

　「英語はむずかしい」とは考えないでください。すべて英語で話さなければいけないなどと考える必要はありません。Business management を英語と日本語の両言語で学びましょう。大切なことは、意味をきちんと伝え合うことです。間違うことを恐れず、Business management という内容を理解することを優先して、英語を使ってください。言語習得のプロセスで間違えない人はいません。従来の英語表現や文法をテストのために学んできた人はCLILスタイルの授業で新しい語学学習を体験してみましょう。

Don't learn English, but use English and do something.

　学習者の英語力は、CEFRの6レベルのB2程度を想定していますが、それぞれの英語レベルに応じて、自律的に学ぶようにしてください。本教科書での学習を通じて、Business management についての学びが深まり、英語でコミュニケーションをする楽しさを感じていただけるよう、著者一同心から願っています。

各 Chapter の構成と学習活動

12 の Chapter と 2 つの Reading で構成されています。各 Chapter の構成と学習活動は次のように想定していますが、自由に柔軟に学んでください。順番どおりに学ぶ必要はありません。興味関心のある内容から学ぶことも可能です。

Warmup
Task 1 Share ideas in English and Japanese
【活動のポイント】英語と日本語で雑談してください。興味関心を高めます。

Familiarize yourself with business words and phrases
Task 2 Brainstorm with your classmates
Task 3 Match each word with the definition
Task 4 Ask each other
Task 5 Send a message on social media using the above words
【活動のポイント】ここでは理解に必要な語句に慣れるようにします。気軽に英語を口にして、語句の使い方に習熟しましょう。

Preview
Task 6 Listen and read
Task 7 Listen and fill in the blanks
Task 8 Share your thoughts in pairs
【活動のポイント】「聞く、話す」ことに集中します。しかし、内容や意味をしっかりと把握しながら読み、話すことにつながるように聞きます。

Topics
Task 9 Read and discuss each question with your classmates
Task 10 What interests you most in this article? Write down your ideas.
【活動のポイント】各 question をもとに考えながら理解を深めるようにしてください。目的はそれぞれのトピックを学ぶことです。和訳や読解をする必要はありません。

Useful words and phrases for business
Task 11 Listen and do shadowing
Task 12 For more details, check an online English-English dictionary
【活動のポイント】ここでは語句の理解の確認と使い方を深めます。オンライン辞書などを使い、それぞれの語句のつながり (collocation) を考え、英語を英語で言い換える力を身につけます。

Research project and discussion
Task 13 Do research …
Task 14 Make a presentation about …
【活動のポイント】柔軟に考えて、興味に合わせてリサーチを楽しむことが大切です。それぞれのトピックに関連する資料を英語と日本語で調べて、それを発表する練習です。ビジネスでは必要なスキルの一つです。

Contents

音声ダウンロード＆ストリーミングサービス（無料）のご案内

https://www.sanshusha.co.jp/text/onsei/isbn/9784384335248/

本書の音声データは、上記アドレスよりダウンロードおよびストリーミング再生ができます。ぜひご利用ください。

Business and our lives

ビジネスと私たちの生活

Warmup

Task 1 **Share ideas in English and Japanese**

Business can mean many things to different people. It might be hard to box it into a single category. Imagine the many different types of businesses you come across in one day. You probably use public transportation to go to university. You may also buy a snack at a stand in the station and use a mobile phone app to search for something.

Q1 When you hear the word 'business,' what is the first thing that comes to your mind?

Q2 What types of business did you see today?

ビジネスをテーマに英語を学びましょう。では、ビジネスとは一体何でしょう？
ビジネスは私たちの生活に根付いたものです。みなさんは、朝起きてから、たくさんの「ビジネス」に触れています。例えば、交通機関、コンビニ、人材派遣、携帯電話等の通信、電気ガス、100円均一ショップ、カフェ、中古品販売、広告、家電の製造、ホテルなど、あげればキリがありません。今日1日で、どのようなビジネスに触れましたか？そして、これらを英語ではなんと言うでしょうか？ビジネスはみなさんの周りを見渡すと、どこにでもあります。早速考えてみましょう。

1. Familiarize yourself with business words and phrases

Business vocabulary is important to our personal and work lives. Business words and phrases are used to describe many things around us such as shopping, sports, traveling, leisure, events, plays, movies, social media, online learning, telecommunication, and technologies.

Task 2 Brainstorm with your classmates

Recall what you did yesterday and tell your classmates about the activities you did. What kind of goods and services did you purchase? Share ideas with your classmates.

e.g. I bought a book on the Internet. I downloaded some music applications.

Task 3 Match each word with the definition

1. earn (*v.*)
2. profit (*n.*)
3. supply (*v.*)
4. intangible (*adj.*)
5. store (*v.*)
6. desire (*v.*)

a. untouchable and abstract
b. to want something
c. money that is made in business or by selling things
d. to keep things in a special place to use later
e. to work and get something for it
f. to give something that people need or want

v. = verb（動詞）   *n.* = noun（名詞）   *adj.* = adjective（形容詞）   *adv.* = adverb（副詞）

Task 4 Ask each other

e.g. A: What does 'earn' mean?
     B: It means to work and get something for it.

Task 5 Send a message on social media using the above words

e.g. I would like to earn a lot of money and be rich.

2. Preview — The role of businesses

001

Task 6 **Listen and read**

A business is an organization that earns a profit by providing goods and services desired by its customers. Goods are tangible items supplied by businesses, such as pens, home appliances, or cars. Services are intangible things provided by businesses that can't be held, touched, or stored, such as hair styling, car washes, flights, and legal services. Businesses fulfill the various needs of customers by providing goods and services with added value. This added value will become a profit.

Q3   What kind of businesses do you want to create?

An example of added value

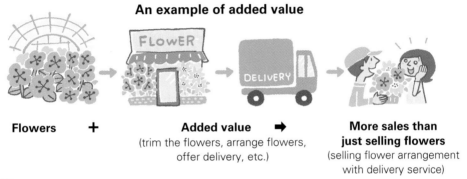

Flowers	**+**	Added value	➡	More sales than
		(trim the flowers, arrange flowers, offer delivery, etc.)		just selling flowers (selling flower arrangement with delivery service)

002

Task 7 **Listen and fill in the blanks**

Creating a new business is not (¹·   ) risks. Risk in business means the (²·   ) to lose time and money. (³·   ), if a company doesn't take risks, it can't achieve its goals. For example, businesses such as fast-food restaurants (⁴·   ) the risk of falling short of their (⁵·   ) and profit goals. Revenue is the money that a (⁶·   ) shop receives by selling burgers and French fries to customers. (⁷·   ) are expenses for running the store: for example, food (⁸·   ) such as bread, meat, cheese, tomatoes for burgers, potatoes for French fries, or many other things that the burger shop has to pay for to (⁹·   ) the business. If the revenue of a burger shop (¹⁰·   ) all the costs, the shop makes a profit, but if the costs are greater than revenues, it will become a loss.

Introduction to Business. OpenStax Rice University (modified).

Task 8 **Share your thoughts in pairs**

Q4   Do you think creating a new business is worth the challenge for you? Why or why not?

e.g.   I don't think it's worth trying because it's too risky.

Q5   If you were the owner of a burger shop, how would you balance revenue and costs? Do you have any good ideas?

e.g.   If I were the owner of a burger shop, I would try....

3. Topics — Starting a business

Task 9 Read and discuss each question with your classmates

003 Businesses play an important role in maintaining our quality of life in areas such as education, health, sanitation, and leisure. In fact, many companies are started by people just like you who want to help other people live better. Starting your own business can be very exciting, but it can also be quite challenging. The following steps will help you understand how to start a business.

Quality of Life
- ☑ education
- ☑ health
- ☑ leisure
- ☑ commuting
- ☑ shopping
- ☑ communication
  ... and more

Q6 What is the first step to starting a business? When you start a business, what do you need to consider most?

004 The very first step of starting a business is to check whether your business idea has the potential to succeed in the market. You have to think about why you want to start the business – you have to visualize the future goal of your business. This will strongly connect to the 'mission' of the company. Then, you have to consider the target customer who would be willing to buy your products or services. Why do you want to sell those products or services to them? You have to think about this question carefully and pursue the market needs for your products or services. At the end of this first step, you need to consider how much cost would be necessary for you to run the business and whether you would have enough sales to make a profit.

Product

Service

Customers

Q7 What do you have to do as the second step when starting a bussiness? Why do you think this step is so important?

005
To achieve the business goal which you decided on in the first step, you have to start thinking about strategies. How you grow your business will depend on how you stack up against your competitors, and how much demand you can create for your products or services. Above all, you have to consider how you can achieve your mission, which should be the future goal of your business. Strategies are these plans to achieve your mission. Defining a business strategy will help you succeed in the market. If there are lots of competitors, creating a strategy leads you to identify your advantages and your ideal position within the market. So, how can you make good strategies? First, you have to analyze the market environment as well as your company's strengths and weaknesses. After that, you can plan activities to create better products and services.

Overview of Management

*'goods' includes products, raw materials, facilities, furniture, etc.

Q8 Who are the stakeholders of your business? Why do you think they are so important?

006
Having a clearly defined mission and strategy will also help you explain your business to other people such as employees or investors, who are also called stakeholders. This is a critical step for seeking financial support and managing human resources. All the stakeholders directly or indirectly influence your business, therefore, keeping good relationships with them is an important factor for the success of your business.

Examples of company stakeholders

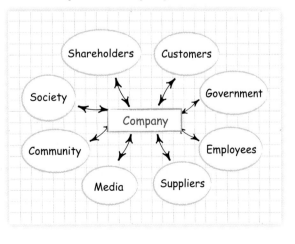

Q9 It is important to manage resources such as people, goods, money, and information. How should you manage them if you start your business?

007

Now you have an idea for a business, and you have set the future goal of your business as a mission of the company. In addition, you have some ideas about your products or services, customers, and competitors. Finally, you are now thinking about how to win against the competitors and reach customers, but you will quickly realize that you need resources such as human resources (people), material resources (goods*), financial resources (money), and intellectual resources (information). Managing these resources is very important – but how should you do it?

Management is the process of creating strategies and designing organizations to achieve a company's long-term goals, which are often stated as the mission of each organization. This involves the efficient distribution of business resources.

* 'goods' includes products, raw materials, facilities, furniture, etc.

Task 10 **What interests you most in this article? Write down your ideas.**

コラム **❶**

ステークホルダーとはだれか

　ステークホルダー(stakeholders)とは「利害関係者」という意味です。企業が活動を行うために関係を持ち、影響を直接的・間接的に及ぼし合う、社会に存在する人々や法人のことを「ステークホルダー」と言います。ステークホルダーは、日本語では「利害関係者」と言い、その「影響し合う」には、良い影響と悪い影響の両方を含みます。例えば、企業にとってお客様(customers)は大切なステークホルダーです。お客様が満足するか否かで、会社の業績は大きく変わるでしょう。また、原料や材料、サービス等を供給してくれる企業(suppliers)や、市場(market)で競争相手となる他企業(competitors)もステークホルダーです。銀行の融資や、原料がなければビジネスの継続は難しいでしょうし、地域住民との良好な関係は、工場の操業のし易さに関わるでしょう。これらのステークホルダーとの関係は非常に重要です。なぜなら、良好な関係、正しい関係を築くことで、企業は安定的でスムーズな経営ができるからです。

4. Useful words and phrases for business

Task 11 **Listen and do shadowing**

words & phrases	sample sentences
fulfill 満たす	He has finally found a job in which he can feel **fulfilled**.
tangible 実体的な	They couldn't accept my findings without **tangible** evidence.
potential 見込みのある	We need to identify actual and **potential** problems.
revenue 総収入	The company's annual **revenue** rose by 30%.
play a key role 重要な役割を果たす	He **plays a key role** in this organization.
sanitation 衛生	A lack of clean water and **sanitation** is a critical problem in the world.
visualize 視覚化する	I can't **visualize** how this project will develop.
consider 熟考する	We are **considering** what we want to do next.
define 定義する	The strategy for this plan should be clearly **defined**.
lead 導く	She tried to **lead** the discussion in a group.
identify 見極める	We could **identify** the main causes of the problem.
stack up 匹敵する	Let's try him on the job and see how he **stacks up**.
added value 付加価値	Considering the **added value** for this project is necessary.
investor 投資家	That **investor** bought up the stocks at once.
critical 重要な	The president thinks it is a **critical** moment for our company.
human resources 人的資源	The manager is responsible for keeping **human resources**.

Task 12 **For more details, check an online English-English dictionary**

1. Use a smartphone or the Internet
2. Select an online English-English dictionary
3. Look up the word(s)
4. Check the results and share ideas with your classmates

5. Research project and discussion

Task 13 **Do research on a business plan in groups**

Guidelines for making your business plan

1. What kind of products or services would you like to sell?
2. Who will buy the products or services?
3. Who are your competitors?
4. Choose one of the social media services you usually use. What is the added value of social media to building a successful business?

Draft of Your Business Plan （事業企画書案）

Your business idea	
1. What kind of products or services would you like to sell?	
2. Who will buy the products or services?	
3. Who are your competitors?	
4. Choose one of the social media you usually use. What is the added value of social media to building a successful business?	

Task 14 **Make a presentation about your business plan**

Which presentation is most impressive?

コラム❷

事業企画書（business plan）

　ビジネスで一番重要なことは、そのビジネスを継続していけるかです。どれくらいそのビジネスに将来性があるか、そして、どれくらいの収益を見込むことができて、事業を継続していくことができるか。この見通しを立てることが重要です。

　そのためには、「何のためにそのビジネスをするのか」「誰のためにするのか」「どのような製品・サービスでその目的を実現するのか」「その製品・サービスは喜ばれて購入されるのか」「すでに同じようなことは行われていないのか」等を想定し、書き起こす必要があります。これが事業企画書の一部となります。もちろん、お金がどれだけいるのか、その投資は回収できるのか、なども想定する必要がありますが、何より「何のために」「誰に」「どのような製品・サービスを」といったことが「ビジネス・アイデア（business idea）」と言われるものであり、ビジネスをスタートするには最も大切なものとなります。

Enterprises and companies

会社とは

Warmup

Task 1 **Share ideas in English and Japanese**

There are many English business terms which are translated into *'Kaisha'* in Japanese: for instance, business, company, firm, enterprise, and corporation. Each company has its purpose for doing business. It is usually stated as a company's mission, vision, and values. The president's message on the company profile webpage is also a good way to know the company's purpose for doing business. Have you ever heard about your favorite company's mission?

Q1   What kind of image do you have when you hear the words like company, firm, or enterprise?

Q2   What do you think about the message of your favorite company's president?

> 会社というとどのようなイメージを持ちますか？スーツを着た人がさっそうと忙しく働いている、身の回りにあるものを作っている……そんなイメージでしょうか？世の中には多くの会社があり、私たちが日々使うもの、食べるもの、様々なものが会社によって提供され、私たちに届けられています。つまり、会社とは社会的な組織であり、その事業により、何かしらの社会の課題解決に貢献していると言えます。そして、その対価として、利益（お金）を得ています。例えば、スーパーでは、野菜や肉・魚などを持ち帰る代わりに、レジでお金を払います。また美容室や理髪店では髪を切ってもらいますが、「髪の毛を切る」というサービスの対価を支払います。このように顧客ニーズに対応し、お金を得ることで会社が成り立ちます。

1. Familiarize yourself with business words and phrases

An enterprise simply refers to a for-profit business or company. You often come across the word 'venture' or 'start-up' when reading about stories of new businesses. There are many types of enterprises.

Task 2 **Brainstorm with your classmates**

Do you want to work at a large enterprise in the future? Or do you want to establish your own company? If you want to start your own company, what company would you establish? Why? If you don't want to, why not? Share your ideas with your classmates.

e.g. I will run a food company in the future. I would like to produce healthy food.
I am more interested in working at large enterprises. I would like to work globally.

Task 3 **Match each word with the definition**

1. start-up (*n.*)
2. corporation (*n.*)
3. commitment (*n.*)
4. condition (*n.*)
5. principles (*n.*)

a. a large company or group of companies under common control
b. a small enterprise that is just beginning to operate
c. a particular state that a person or thing is in
d. being actively involved in a business/company
e. a set of basic rules or ideas that tell how something happens or works

Task 4 **Ask each other**

e.g. A: What does 'corporation' mean?
B: It means …

Task 5 **Send a message on social media using the above words**

e.g. Nowadays, many young people are interested in IT start-ups.

2. Preview — Part-time or full-time

009

Task 6 **Listen and read**

What conditions are necessary for you to take a part-time job? Are these the same conditions to work full-time in the future? Each company usually has its mission and vision statements. Employees working there are supposed to understand them and are expected to show their commitment to the company. People who work in a company they like often stay longer than others who don't, and the company also benefits from that situation.

Q3 Do you know why the company would benefit if you worked longer in it?

010

Task 7 **Listen and fill in the blanks**

($^{1.}$) should provide equal pay for equal work. The hourly rate for part-time and full-time ($^{2.}$) should be the same when they do the same work. Currently, more people in the UK are working part-time than ever ($^{3.}$). It is said that nearly one in four employees work 30 or ($^{4.}$) hours a week these days. Which will you ($^{5.}$), full-time or part-time work? Your decision will be ($^{6.}$) for you, your family, and your future ($^{7.}$). There is no right or ($^{8.}$) decision. It is just a ($^{9.}$) of deciding what will work ($^{10.}$) for you.

Task 8 **Share your thoughts in pairs**

Q4 Do you agree that employees should be expected to understand their company's purpose, principles, mission, and vision?

e.g. I don't think so. I just want to work for myself.

Q5 What image do you have of a typical office worker? Explain why you have this image.

e.g. An office worker is a person wearing a suit and working at an office for many hours.

3. Topics — A mission-driven company

Task 9 Read and discuss each question with your classmates

011 A company is often driven by a mission, aiming to solve a specific problem. It uses its mission statement to clearly define the need for as well as its path to a solution. The mission statement may be the right place to get started, but being mission-driven may be fuzzy. Many companies say they are mission-driven. However, people doubt whether it is true or not. Many people may not know what 'mission-driven' really means. Even if a company has a mission statement, it doesn't necessarily mean it is a mission-driven company.

Q6 Why do companies have missions? How do you like mission-driven companies?

012 A company carries out its business solely driven by its business opportunity. Some companies were established because the founder thought of a way to make money, but most business opportunities are related to the unrealized needs of customers. From this point of view, we can say that all companies have the goal to achieve

or provide some kinds of solutions to customers. This could be the base of their corporate missions. Awareness of the concrete reason why a company exists will make business management easier, as the goal of the business is clear. The mission may also add another reason to believe in the company's greater purpose. It often describes some social good that is detached from what the company actually produces. Those companies which have a clear mission and make their business decisions along with it are called 'mission-driven companies.'

Q7 How does the corporate mission work for a company and its employees? Do you know any companies which do social good?

013 A company is usually started to solve some unrevealed needs of people. Once a business gets on track, it tries to solve them in bigger and better ways. In such situations, the corporate mission is an important direction to develop products and services which fit the company. What is more, if all the employees in a company understand its mission, they can focus on business and commit more fully to the work. The mission can help employees understand the company's goals and obstacles. It is a huge advantage for a mission-driven company to be able to make business decisions more quickly in order to stay on track for the future.

Q8 What do you think about company missions? Do you understand how important it is for a company?

014 A company mission is a long-term goal of a company, so it does not change so often. What a company builds today might not be what it will build tomorrow. Products, services, technologies, and people working at a company will change over time, but its mission does not change so easily. Whenever companies go through business activities early on, they will ask themselves a lot of questions they might otherwise not get to answer soon. But these questions are all important for them to ask in order to find, refine, and articulate their missions. The company mission may be hard to define, but it has a great influence on company management. It could be a strong tool to help a company create better products and services, develop a stronger culture, and enhance resilience so that it might survive for a long time.

Q9 How does a mission statement work for a company? Is it necessary for every company?

015 The mission statement of each company presents its long-term goal, so it naturally follows the path of the founder's spirit and the company's history. The mission statement itself determines a company's business domains, which are the competitive boundaries that influence their strategic choices and performance. It ultimately clarifies a company's business direction, which includes what kinds of products and services the company offers to their markets and customers.

Q10 Which coffee shop do you want to go, Café NANA or Café COCO? Why?

016 As told above, companies provide a variety of products and services connecting to their missions, and they get paid by the customers who buy products and services. To start any business, the company or corporate mission statement, which shows what a company or corporation would like to achieve, is extremely important. See the tables below. There are two cafés, both of which sell similar products, but they have different mission statements.

The mission statements of Café NANA and Café COCO

Café NANA	Café COCO
"Our mission is to serve aromatic specialty coffee to provide comfort in customers' daily lives"	"Our mission is to serve tasty coffee at an appropriate price during workers' break time"

The management details of Café NANA and Café COCO

	Café NANA	Café COCO
Target customers	• Trend-conscious, people who have time • People who want to drink coffee in a cozy atmosphere • People who like specialty coffee	• Business people • People who want to enjoy coffee quickly at a reasonable price
Location	Suburbs, trendy places in the city	Stations, business areas
Atmosphere	Sofas, comfortable chairs, a lot of green, terrace	Standing, bar style counters, 2-seaters
Open hours	10:00 to 20:00	From early morning to late night
Employees & hospitality	Enough numbers of staff to give time-intensive and exceptional services with good knowledge of specialty coffee and a high level of politeness	Minimum but well-trained staff for quick and effective services

Task 10   **What interests you most in this article? Write down your ideas.**

コラム❶   **企業理念とは**

　企業理念は、その企業のビジネスにおける目的・価値観を示します。また、その企業が何のために、どのようにビジネスを行うのかを示したものです。企業の経営観が反映されているため、企業理念はビジネスの方向性や判断の基準となります。多くの企業はその理念を公表し、目指すゴールを社会に明確に示しています。このように企業理念は、将来にわたっての企業のあり方を示すので、社員がそれを理解しておくことはとても重要です。企業理念に共感していれば、社員はその会社で働くことに大きな「やりがい」を感じることができるでしょう。

4. Useful words and phrases for business

Task 11 **Listen and do shadowing**

017

words & phrases	sample sentences
mission 使命	The main **mission** of ABC company is to help people.
mission statement ミッションステートメント	Most companies have a **mission statement**.
mission-driven ミッションによる	**Mission-driven** businesses can change the world.
social good 社会に良いこと	Robots have great potential for **social good**.
founder 創設者	Ms. Yamaguchi is the **founder** of the company.
aim 目的	The **aim** of this project is to donate to people in poverty.
define 定義する	It's necessary to **define** this technical term.
get started 取りかかる	Today's meeting will **get started** in the morning.
carry out 実行する	Our manager decided to **carry out** this project.
fall into 落ちる	Many people **fell into** poverty after the depression.
focus on 注目する	We should **focus on** this topic immediately.
stay on track 順調に物事を進める	Set a timer to **stay on track** during the meeting.
adapt to 適応する	Companies must **adapt to** the current situation.
go through 詳細に見直す	Let's **go through** the agenda again.

Task 12 **For more details, check an online English-English dictionary**

1. Use a smartphone or the Internet
2. Select an online English-English dictionary
3. Look up the word(s)
4. Check the results and share ideas with your classmates

5. Research project and discussion

Task 13 ## Do research on a mission statement in groups

How is a company's mission statement related to its business? Choose one enterprise or company and research the mission statement relating to the products or services.

> The Corporate Statement* of USJ LLC
>
> The corporate statement of USJ LLC is "Energizing people and society with super entertaining creativity."
>
> We think USJ LLC's Corporate Statement is related to their business because they are providing exciting experiences to the customers such as rides with advanced technologies.....

Source: https://www.usj.co.jp/company/about/vision.html

*USJ LLC（Universal Studios Japan の運営会社）は、「存在意義」を表す言葉として "Corporate Statement" を使用している（コラム②参照）。

Task 14 ## Make a presentation on a mission statement

Which presentation is most impressive?

コラム ②

企業理念の重要性

　企業理念は、会社の規模によらず存在します（なお、企業理念を公にしていない場合もあり、コーポレート・ステートメントやミッション、フィロソフィーといった別の呼び方で設定している場合もあります）。例として、産業用機械を製造する大手企業ヤンマーホールディングス株式会社のミッションステートメントを見てみましょう。そこには「食料生産とエネルギー変換の分野でより豊かな暮らしを実現する」とあります。ヤンマーホールディングス株式会社は農業機械でも有名ですが、これはミッションの食料生産の部分に関わると考えられます。また、株式会社ゴエンジンはスタートアップの小さな会社ですが、企業理念は「より良いコミュニケーションを創ることで、よりステキな毎日をより多くの人々に」です。さて、ゴエンジンは何の会社か想像できますか？答えは、広告・宣伝やイベントの企画サポートで、人々や企業のコミュニケーションに関わる内容です。いかに企業理念がビジネスと直結しているかがわかりますね。

ヤンマーホールディングス㈱の
ミッションステートメント

わたしたちは
自然と共生し
生命の根幹を担う
食料生産とエネルギー変換の分野で
お客様の課題を解決し
未来につながる社会と
より豊かな暮らしを実現します。

株式会社ゴエンジンのミッション

MISSION
使命

より良いコミュニケーションを創ることで、よりステキな毎日をより多くの人々に

Strategy 1:
The PESTLE analysis

ストラテジー1　PESTLE分析

Warmup

Task 1 **Share ideas in English and Japanese**

What you want to accomplish is your mission, and the vision is a general statement of how you will achieve it. Strategies are a series of ways to achieve this mission and vision. Environment analysis is the study of external environmental factors related to businesses. Let's learn about PESTLE analysis, a type of external environmental analyses.

Q1　What is the biggest outside factor influencing food companies today? Why do you think so?

Q2　To set a business strategy for a food business, what aspects of the market do you have to analyze?

企業理念（ミッション）は会社が長期的に目指すものです。ミッション主導型の会社は、それを判断基準の軸として、迅速に新しいアイデアやチャンスに対応できることが大きな利点です。企業がどのように市場で戦っていくかに必要な意思決定を、「戦略（strategy）」と言います。その戦略を作るための環境分析の1つにPESTLE分析があります。

1. Familiarize yourself with business words and phrases

Two hamburger shops are selling hamburgers in the market. One is a big hamburger chain, and the other is a small, personally owned shop loved by local people. These two shops have their missions and visions. Their strategies are of course different.

Task 2 Brainstorm with your classmates

Which kind of hamburger shop do you often go to? Why do you go there? Which factors do you value, brand image, taste, or price? Share ideas with your classmates and compare yours with theirs.

e.g. I usually go to a big hamburger chain. I just choose based on price and taste.

Task 3 Match each word with the definition

1. market (*n.*)
2. achieve (*v.*)
3. strategy (*n.*)
4. goal (*n.*)
5. analyze (*v.*)

a. an aim set to achieve the objectives
b. a detailed plan to accomplish a particular purpose
c. to identify and examine carefully
d. the business place where sellers and consumers freely buy and sell various goods
e. to accomplish a certain aim

Task 4 Ask each other

e.g. A: What does 'goal' mean?
B: It means ...

Task 5 Send a message on social media using the above words

e.g. My goal for this year is to improve my English.

2. Preview — A market analysis

Task 6 Listen and read

018

Before any kind of strategy is planned, it is essential to conduct a market analysis. One of the most popular market analyses is called a **PESTLE analysis**. It stands for six external factors which need to be considered: Political, Economic, Sociological, Technological, Legal, and Environmental. A PESTLE analysis is a useful tool to identify changes in an industry environment. Companies should analyze all these factors to gain insight into the external influences which may impact their strategy and business plans.

Q3 Which factor of the PESTLE analysis do you think is most likely to affect the start of a new business? Which factor is most interesting to you?

Task 7 Listen and fill in the blanks

019

Risa (R): Hi, Koji. I am thinking about opening a café near your university. What do you think?

Koji (K): That's a great (1.   ), but I suggest you analyze the external factors before making a (2.   ) decision.

R: The external factors? What do you mean? Why is it necessary to (3.   ) them? What kinds of factors are they?

WE ARE OPEN!
COFFEE SHOP

COFFEE

K: I mean the external factors relating to your (4.   ), such as political, economic, sociological, technological, legal, and environmental factors. Have you heard about the PESTLE analysis?

R: I'm afraid not, but (5.   ) factors might be related to the café market, right?

K: Yeah. Let's learn about the PESTLE analysis. It will be (6.   ) when starting your business.

Task 8 Share your thoughts in pairs

Q4 Which kind of business are you interested in, fashion, delivery, travel, technology, or something else?

e.g. I am interested in car dealerships, and I think it is important to think about future sources of energy.

Q5 Which external factors of the PESTLE analysis are important for you to be successful in that business?

e.g. Environmental factors are most important when developing a car.

3. Topics — The PESTLE analysis

Task 9 Read and discuss each question with your classmates

020
In a market, many companies compete against each other by trying to sell more products and services. In order to sell more, companies must try to lower their prices and increase the quality of products, which keeps their profits modest. This means that companies must work hard to stand out from other companies if they want to earn larger profits.

Q6 How does the market environment relate to business strategy?

021
Analyzing the market environment is a key part of the strategy-making process. Many tools can be utilized to help define what information to collect. One of these tools is a framework called a PESTLE analysis. It can be used to understand the impact of outside factors on a business or organization.

Q7 What can a PESTLE analysis contribute to companies?

022
A PESTLE analysis allows companies to understand the 'overview' of the market situation they are playing in. Using a PESTLE analysis, a company can evaluate a business's prospects, risks, and opportunities in a market strategically as well as systematically. The PESTLE analysis can be used for not only comparing the situations between companies but also analyzing small-scale in-house projects.

Q8 What factors do you have to especially consider while using a PESTLE analysis?

023
In a PESTLE analysis, a company considers six external market factors — Political, Economic, Social, Technological, Legal, and Environmental — influencing the project or the company itself. Don't forget that these PESTLE factors need to be related to the company's specific operational project. It is very important to emphasize some specific factors that could impact your business project and focus your analysis on them.

Q9 What are some specific examples of a PESTLE analysis?

024
Whenever you conduct a PESTLE analysis, you need to consider each factor separately. First, political (P) factors include political risks such as the stability of the country's government, wars, public welfare policies, trade regulations, or any trading agreements the country is involved in, such as the Regional Comprehensive Economic Partnership (RCEP). Economic (E) factors include the raw material cost, the economic climate, unemployment rates, interest rates, and current exchange rates. Some examples of sociocultural (S) factors are population demographics, religion and ethics, media, and trends regarding work and lifestyles. When considering

technological (T) factors, companies may think about new or innovative technologies influencing the company or project, such as new mobile devices, ICT (Information and Communication Technology), AI (Artificial Intelligence), patents, or automation. As for legal (L) factors, companies have to think about regulations such as employment laws, environmental regulations, and consumer protections. These legal factors can affect the policies and procedures of each company. Finally, environmental (E) factors include the climate, pollution, and energy. They are critical for all industries because investors, as well as people in our society, care more about such environmental issues than before.

Q10　What are PESTLE factors for Risa's new business (Task 7)?

 025 The figure below shows an example of a PESTLE analysis for Risa's new coffee shop near the university, which you heard about in Task 7. Can you think of other examples regarding Risa's new business?

The PESTLE analysis for Risa's coffee shop

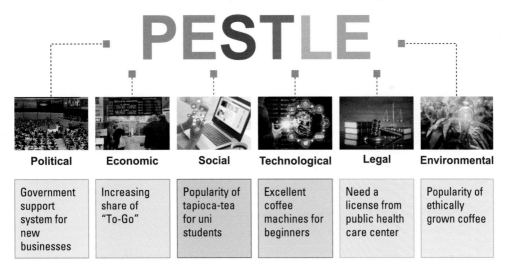

Political	Economic	Social	Technological	Legal	Environmental
Government support system for new businesses	Increasing share of "To-Go"	Popularity of tapioca-tea for uni students	Excellent coffee machines for beginners	Need a license from public health care center	Popularity of ethically grown coffee

Task 10 **What interests you most in this article? Write down your ideas.**

You need to conduct a PESTLE analysis for your business

E
Economic
- economic growth
- employment rates
- monetary policy
- consumer confidence

S
Social
- income distribution
- demographic influence
- lifestyle factors
- media opinions

P
Political
- stability of government
- potential changes to legislation
- global influence

T
Technological
- international influence
- changes in information technology
- take up rates

E
Environmental
- regulations and restrictions
- stakeholders and customers values
- climates

L
Legal
- taxation policies
- employment laws
- industry regulations
- health and safety

コラム ❶

外部環境分析（external environmental analysis）とは

　会社（companies, firms）は社会の中に存在しつつ、私たちの日々の生活に大きく影響を与えます。また、会社は社会の様々な状況（外部環境）に影響を受けます。そのため、経営においては、様々な社会の変化に目を向けることも必要です。では、経営に影響する外部環境とはどのようなものでしょう。例えば、少子高齢化が進めば、子供が対象のビジネスは難しくなります。健康志向が高まれば、カロリーの低いお菓子が売れるでしょう。このような外部環境の分析にはPESTLE分析を用います。経営を取り巻く環境をP（Politics: 政治）、E（Economy: 経済）、S（Social: 社会情勢）、T（Technology: 技術）、L（Laws: 法律）、E（Environment: 環境）に分類し、その影響を分析します。

4. Useful words and phrases for business

Task 11 **Listen and do shadowing**

026

words & phrases	sample sentences
fundamental 基本の	**Fundamental** rules are necessary for a company.
external 外的の	In a PESTLE analysis, there are six **external** market factors.
sociological 社会学的な	This strategy was based on **sociological** studies.
legal 法律に関する	Our company received **legal** advice from a lawyer.
confirm 確認する	I **confirmed** their attendance at the meeting.
differentiation 差別化	**Differentiation** makes this tea attractive.
profits 利益	Our company had quite a lot of **profit** this year.
modest 控えめな	We have only a **modest** budget for this project.
strategic 戦略上の	It is always important to conduct a detailed **strategic** analysis.
systematic 系統的な	The presenter was asked to provide a **systematic** explanation.
relevance 関連性	We were not able to understand the **relevance** of these problems.
stability 安定	Most managers think first and foremost about business **stability**.
trade agreement 貿易協定	They signed the **trade agreement**.
unemployment 失業	The **unemployment** rate decreased from 4.0% to 3.8%.
demographic 人口統計学の	We can learn a lot from **demographic** statistics.
innovative 革新的な	His idea was so **innovative** that we adopted it.

Task 12 **For more details, check an online English-English dictionary**

1. Use a smartphone or the Internet
2. Select an online English-English dictionary
3. Look up the word(s)
4. Check the results and share ideas with your classmates

5. Research project and discussion

Task 13 Conduct a PESTLE analysis in groups

Suppose you are starting a new business to sell hand-made soap on the Internet.
Analyze the business environment of the soap market with the PESTLE analysis.
Guidelines for the analysis

1. Who is your target customer?
2. What factors in PESTLE do you need to consider to sell hand-made soap?
3. What factor is most important?

		Examples	Let's try!
P	Political	Stability of countries Tax policies Trade agreements	➢ Local government's support for entrepreneurs
E	Economical	Economic climate Unemployment rate Current exchange rate	➢ Grant for starting a business ➢ Suitable currency exchange rate for the business
S	Social / Cultural	Trends Media Demographics	➢ Hand-made soap is in fashion
T	Technological	New technologies New devices ICT/ AI	➢ Easy to make without specific technology
L	Legal	Regulations Court system Labor laws	➢ The legal advantage of self-employment (e.g. progressive taxation)
E	Environmental	Climate change Waste management Energy / Environmental protection	➢ Popularity of eco-friendly products

Task 14 Make a presentation about your PESTLE analysis

Which presentation is most impressive?

コラム ❷

戦略 (strategy) とは何か

　ビジネスにおける戦略 (strategy) とは、その会社が市場でどうやって競合他社と戦っていくかを理論的に組み立てた方策と言えるでしょう。この方策が成功すれば、市場での地位を確立できますし、そうでなければそのビジネスの継続は難しくなるかもしれません。戦略立案のためには、外部環境や、その会社の置かれる状況分析をしっかりと行い、俯瞰することが必要です。なお、戦略にはその会社がどの分野で戦っていくか等、大きな方向性を決める「企業戦略」と、その展開を決めた事業において、どうやって競争優位を見出すのかという「事業戦略」があります。さらに、それらの戦略をどう具体的に実現していくかを「戦術」と言います。

Chapter 4

Strategy 2: The SWOT analysis

ストラテジー2　SWOT 分析

Warmup

Task 1 Share ideas in English and Japanese

You learned how to conduct a PESTLE analysis, so you have begun to understand its necessity and importance. Every company needs a clear strategy to grow its business. To further analyze your business, you need more methods of analysis. For instance, the SWOT analysis is useful.

Q1 If you started your own business, what kind of added value would you want to offer customers to achieve your goals?

Q2 It would be helpful to learn more types of business analyses. What else should you consider or analyze to make a strategy?

企業は社会的な存在であり、社会の変化を敏感にキャッチすることが必要です。一例として、PESTLE という外部環境の分析方法では、その変化を確認し、自社は何ができるのかを考えます。また、自社が現在持っている「強み」と「弱み」、そして、「チャンス（機会）」と「脅威」をまとめる枠組み（フレームワーク）のひとつに、SWOT分析があります。これらの分析が戦略立案につながります。

1. Familiarize yourself with business words and phrases

When you buy clothes, do you go to brick-and-mortar stores, which are traditional stores that you find in the city or your local shopping mall, or online stores?

Task 2 Brainstorm with your classmates

Which do you choose to shop at, brick-and-mortar stores or online stores? Share your ideas with your classmates and compare your answers.

e.g. I often buy my clothes at a familiar brick-and-mortar store, because I can try them on to find my size.

I prefer an online store these days because it is more convenient.

Task 3 Match each word with the definition

1. current (*adj.*)
2. strength (*n.*)
3. weakness (*n.*)
4. opportunity (*n.*)
5. threat (*n.*)
6. competitor (*n.*)

a. intimidation or fear using force
b. ongoing or present-day
c. a person who participates in a competition
d. strong physical or mental characteristics
e. the quality of lacking power
f. a chance to do something

Task 4 Ask each other

e.g. A: What does 'current' mean?
　　　 B: It means ...

Task 5 Send a message on social media using the above words

e.g. It was a great opportunity to meet the CEO of our company at the party.

2. Preview — Competitive advantage in markets

027

Task 6 Listen and read

Every company needs a clear strategy to grow its business. To continue analyzing your business from various perspectives, you need to learn another common framework called the SWOT analysis, which is useful for strategic planning. SWOT stands for **strengths** (S), **weaknesses** (W), **opportunities** (O), and **threats** (T). This analysis helps you look at the internal and external factors that can influence your business. The internal factors include the strengths and weaknesses of your business, whereas the external factors are the threats and opportunities. The SWOT analysis is not only useful for identifying strengths or weaknesses, but it can also help you find opportunities for making bigger profits. Opportunities can be found in external factors, such as new consumer trends or new technologies. On the other hand, the external factors that cause problems for your business are called "threats," and include things such as competitors' new products and advertisement campaigns.

Q3   Do you think the SWOT analysis would be useful for you to start your business?

028

Task 7 Listen and fill in the blanks

Jun (J): Hi, Taka. You look nice today. Are those a new pair of shoes?

Taka (T): Yes! I really like them. They are very ($^{1.}$) to walk in.

J: Where did you buy them?

T: Actually, I ($^{2.}$) them at an online store.

J: I can't believe that! I always buy shoes at the shoe store near my house. Trying them on is a ($^{3.}$) when I buy a pair of shoes.

T: I used to think so, but the online store lets me upload my pictures. The app ($^{4.}$) measures my feet and suggests just the right size.

J: Umm…new technologies provide a wide ($^{5.}$) of opportunities for online stores, don't they? It is a big ($^{6.}$) to traditional shoe stores.

Task 8 Share your thoughts in pairs

Q4   What do you think about the strength of highly-recognized brands?

e.g.   They can sell their products globally. This is a strength.

Q5   What do you think about some recent changes to the business environment?

e.g.   Many people go home earlier and eat dinner with their family. This might be a big threat to restaurants.

3. Topics — The SWOT analysis

Task 9 Read and discuss each question with your classmates

029 You can use a SWOT analysis at any stage of your business development. Seeing strengths and weaknesses as internal factors and opportunities and threats as external factors will guide you to solutions for the future of your business and clarify what actions to take.

Q6 What are the factors you consider when conducting a SWOT analysis?

030 The most effective way to conduct a SWOT analysis is to list your perspectives for strengths (S), weaknesses (W), opportunities (O), and threats (T) and assess these together as a holistic view of your business. It is important to clearly distinguish 'internal' things that can impact and directly influence your business from 'external' things that can influence but don't directly impact your business. Strengths and weaknesses are internal factors for companies, while opportunities and threats are always external factors for them. See the 2 x 2 matrix as shown below. It is often used for conducting a SWOT analysis.

S *Simply what the firm is good at*	**W** *Simply what the firm is NOT good at*
O *Environmental factors which are good for the firm*	**T** *Environmental factors which are NOT good for the firm*

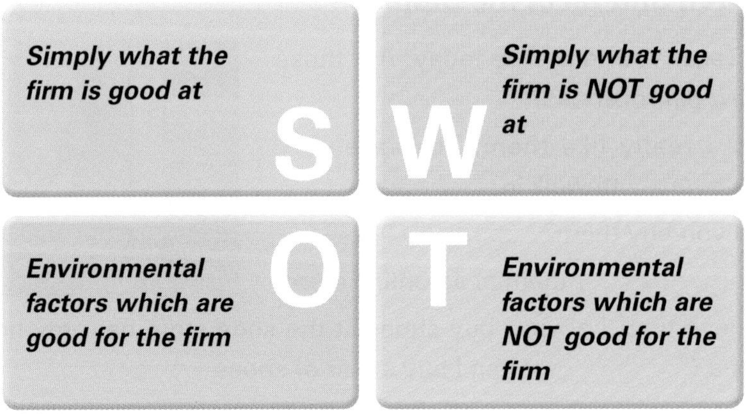

コラム ❶ SWOT 分析 (SWOT analysis) とは

　ビジネスでは客観的な視点が必要不可欠です。SWOT 分析では、視点を少し変え、自社 (のビジネス) の強み (Strengths)、弱み (Weaknesses)、機会 (Opportunities)、脅威 (Threats) を考えます。ネットスーパーを例にとると、強みは「家で生鮮食料品の買い物ができる」ということです。一方で、生鮮食料品は、注文を受けてから迅速に配達する必要があるので「配達コストと人員の確保」は弱みです。機会は、「超高齢化社会によりニーズが増えそうなこと」、脅威は、「農家直送の生鮮食料品の定期配送など」が考えられます。なお、そのビジネスを代替する新しいテクノロジーなども脅威と位置づけます。

Q7 Do you watch TV? What do you think of the future of TV broadcasting?

031
As mentioned above, a SWOT analysis is a structured and detailed way to evaluate the strengths, weaknesses, opportunities, and threats involved in the business. Next, you will consider some strategies for using a SWOT analysis. First, let's start by identifying what strengths, weaknesses, opportunities, and threats are present in the TV broadcasting business. Imagine your daily life. Right after waking up in the

morning, what kind of media do you access first? Maybe each of you uses different devices to access different media. For example, someone may read a newspaper, or someone may watch morning TV shows, and many will check social media. It is necessary to access media somehow to obtain new or updated information about our society.

Q8 What types of factors influence a TV broadcasting company?

032
Nowadays we have more varied ways to access a large amount of information, but we can surprisingly see that information provided by TV programs still has enormous power and influence on people in modern society. Look at the figure below. You can understand what types of factors influence a TV broadcasting company based on a SWOT analysis: strengths (S), weaknesses (W), opportunities (O), and threats (T).

SWOT for a TV broadcasting company

Strengths (S):
- TV programs can reach people in various generations at one time
- Easy to reach to many people at one time
- Many people turn on the TV without any intension to watch anything in particular
- Contents are easily publicized
- TV broadcasting companies have already accumulated their own popular contents

Weaknesses (W):
- Need a TV as a machine to watch
- No strong reach to teenagers and people in their 20s
- The internet can be reached via various devices such as smart phones, tablets, and computers
- TV programs are broadcast on a fixed time schedule

Opportunities (O):
- Japan is an aging society, so access to TV programs could increase
- More and more parents prefer to spend time with family members even in the evening on weekdays, so TV could be a good activity for sharing time with family

Threats (T):
- Some companies have started to provide high quality content (dramas, movies, comedies, etc.) through their own internet sites with subscriptions
- It is possible that the electric companies will stop manufacturing TVs due to the shrinking number of customers who buy them

Q9 How can you use the SWOT analysis to plan strategies for the future?

033 Considering and evaluating the SWOT analysis results, a company will decide its strategies from the combination of those SWOT factors. There are 4 major patterns of combinations.

1. S-O: The company selects strategies to create opportunities using its strengths.
2. S-T: The company clarifies how to use its strengths to avoid threats.
3. W-O: The company considers how to overcome its weaknesses to avoid lost opportunities.
4. W-T: The company envisions the worst-case scenario when its weaknesses and threats come together.

In these ways, the SWOT analysis is a strong tool to formulate strategies for the future.

Q10 What kinds of factors should you consider while using the strategic analysis?

034 How can a TV broadcasting company perform better in the future based on the SWOT analysis? The factors analyzed by SWOT are related to each other. For instance, a TV broadcasting company can use its strengths (S) to overcome its weaknesses (W) or threats (T), or it can think about how it can make use of opportunities (O) while defending its strengths (S). If you were the owner of a TV broadcasting company, what strategies would you use to expand the audience? In any kind of business, it is critical to analyze the business environment (e.g. PESTLE) or internal resources and market prospects (e.g. SWOT). Now you may find it interesting to read or watch economic news to get to know the new business challenges. For example, why did car companies start manufacturing electric cars? Or why are online supermarkets still not very popular? Pay more attention to these analytical strategies while planning for your business.

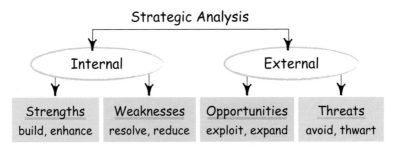

Task 10 **What interests you most in this article? Write down your ideas.**

4. Useful words and phrases for business

035

Task 11 **Listen and do shadowing**

words & phrases	sample sentences
aspect 面、見地	There are many **aspects** to consider about this problem.
internal 内在的な	We should inspect an **internal** part of our organization.
external 対外的な	That NGO needs **external** support.
consumer trends 消費者動向	The data accurately shows the **consumer trends** in Japan.
counteract 逆らう、(反作用で)中和する	The exercise **counteracted** the employee's stress.
perspectives 考え方、見方	We have to broaden our **perspectives**.
holistic 全体論の、全体の	Our manager gave a **holistic** view of our business.
assess 評価する、査定する	The real estate company **assessed** the value of our old house.
access アクセスする、利用する	Our students have **access** to a library on this campus.
obtain 得る	We tried to **obtain** permission to design a new product.
update 最新のものにする	The secretary **updated** the president's schedule.
perform 行う、実行する	He needs to **perform** his duty as a politician.
prospect 予想、見通し	It is always important to consider new business **prospects**.

Task 12 **For more details, check an online English-English dictionary**

1. Use a smartphone or the Internet
2. Select an online English-English dictionary
3. Look up the word(s)
4. Check the results and share ideas with your classmates

5. Research project and discussion

Task 13　Conduct a SWOT analysis in groups

Choose one company and conduct a SWOT analysis. Make sure to use the 2 x 2 matrix for your analysis, listing strengths, weaknesses, opportunities, and threats.

Guidelines (useful questions)

What things does the company do well?
Where does the company have fewer resources than its competitors?
What market opportunities are present for the company?
How do the company's weaknesses expose it to threats?

Strengths (S):

Weaknesses (W):

Opportunities (O):

Threats (T):

Task 14　Make a presentation about your SWOT analysis

Which presentation is most impressive?

コラム ❷　　　　ビジネスの脅威はライバル会社だけではない！？

　　SWOT分析を行うと、脅威の部分は、自社のビジネスに関して直接的なものだけを考えがちです。しかし、想像力を働かすと、脅威とは決して直接的なものだけではありません。例えば、オンライン会議が一般的になった今、海外出張が大幅に減っていくだろうと考えられます。オンライン会議が一般的になる前は、飛行機のビジネスユースは、航空会社にとって収益の大きな柱の１つだったはずです。しかし、オンライン会議のクオリティが格段に上がってきたことに加え、外部環境の変化もあり、このテクノロジーは今や航空会社にとって大きな脅威であるはずです。このように、将来起こり得ることを想像力豊かに考えてみることは、既存のビジネスを守るため、また新たなビジネスチャンスを創造するためにとても大切です。突飛なアイデアを歓迎する、という風潮がビジネス界にあるのはこのためです。

Chapter 5

Resource management

経営資源とは

Warmup

Task 1 Share ideas in English and Japanese

Resource management in businesses is the practice of planning, acquiring, allocating, and managing resources. In Japan, human resources (people); material resources (goods*) such as facilities, equipment, and products; financial resources (money); and intellectual resources (information) are four major resources for companies. If you start your business, you need to think about how to manage those four major internal resources.

* 'goods' includes products, raw materials, facilities, furniture, etc.

Q1 What categories of resources do you think are most important?

Q2 One example of a financial resource is funding. What are some examples from the other 3 categories: human, material, and information resources? Which specific resources can you think of?

企業が市場で競争して利益をあげるために、何をすればよいかという「戦略」を立てるにあたっては、政治や経済、社会、技術、法律、環境といった、企業活動に大きな影響を与える外部環境の分析（PESTLE分析）、そして自社の強みや弱み、また市場における機会や脅威の分析（SWOT分析）が不可欠です。さらに、企業が今、どんな資源（その企業が自由に使えるリソース）を保持しているのかを知ることも重要です。なお、企業には、4つの資源があると言われてきました。「ヒト human resources（people）・モノ material resources（goods）・カネ financial resources（money）・情報 intellectual resources（information）」です。なお、企業の資源としての「モノ」には、製品や原材料だけではなく、装置や家具なども含まれます。

1. Familiarize yourself with business words and phrases

There are tangible and intangible resources. Tangible resources are visible things including cash, land, and buildings. Intangible resources are not visible and include patents, trademarks, and copyrights.

Task 2 Brainstorm with your classmates

Classify the words below into two different groups: tangible and intangible resources. Write them in the boxes below. Share your ideas with your classmates and compare your answers with theirs.

> email   PC   photocopier   patent   paper   brand image
> chairs   buildings   technical information   intellectual property

Tangible resources	Intangible resources

Task 3 Match each word with the definition

1. distribute (v.)
2. tangible (adj.)
3. resources (n.)
4. inventory (n.)
5. credit (n.)

a. the status of being approved and trusted
b. can be touched and perceived
c. goods and raw materials that are temporarily stored
d. to give something out to people
e. things available to be used for human life, industry, and other activities

Task 4 Ask each other

e.g. A: What does 'credit' mean?
      B: It means ...

Task 5 Send a message on social media using the above words

e.g. The local magazine was distributed freely.

2. Preview — Important decision-making

036

Task 6 **Listen and read**

It is important for a company to know how many resources it distributes to each business section, but it is always difficult to do so. Imagine you are a member of the management team of a bookstore chain. You may want to distribute a larger amount of business resources to keep current sales and profits in the retail section of a physical bookstore that still produces the most sales for your company. However, considering the future, you may feel that the company should use more resources for its e-commerce or online section. Decision-making for resource distribution is always difficult, and it is, therefore, necessary to analyze the business situation well.

Q3 Which do you like better, a physical bookstore or an online bookstore?

037

Task 7 **Listen and fill in the blanks**

No Budget increase !!

Koji (K): How was the budget meeting?

Risa (R): It was awful. In ($^{1.}$) years, the sales of my department have been quite ($^{2.}$), so I expected the budget to increase for the next ($^{3.}$) year, but actually it will be reduced.

K: Oh no, that's too bad. Did you hear the reason?

R: The management team would like to ($^{4.}$) more of the budget to the new department. They feel the business of my department has ($^{5.}$). They think our company needs to ($^{6.}$) more in the new business.

K: It will take several years for the new business to ($^{7.}$) revenue, so I can understand their decision.

R: In addition, they told me two of my colleagues will move to the new department. It will be a big ($^{8.}$) of human resources.

Task 8 **Share your thoughts in pairs**

Q4 Do you have any favorite brands? Why do you like them?

e.g. One of the brands that I like is LEXUS because everybody can recognize it is a high-status brand.

Q5 Which resources are most important if you run your own company?

e.g. I think employees are most important because I can achieve goals that I couldn't reach on my own.

3. Topics — Managing business resources

Task 9 Read and discuss each question with your classmates

038
What do you think of when you hear the word 'resources'? Some may think of oil, gold, or water, and others may think of fish, forests, or soil. For enterprises or companies, 'resources' means everything used by them to achieve their long- and short-term goals. It is key to think about how to distribute resources to survive as a profitable company. Moreover, the resources available will directly influence their competitive advantages when starting a new business.

Q6 What are the resources available for an IT start-up called Z Ltd.? What are the important management resources for that company?

039

Imagine you are an entrepreneur and Chief Executive Officer (CEO) of an IT start-up called Z Ltd. You rent a small office and own 10 PCs for 10 people. You hire another 9 people and have two-million yen as a running cost this month. The sales, profit, and costs of your company are quite stable every month. The company was founded one year ago with a capital of 5 million yen. One of your employees has developed a new security software program. Your company has a technical patent for this software and has sold 1,000 units. Now you are thinking about developing new gaming software, so you are planning to hire two part-time workers. Seeing this situation, can you identify the important management resources?

Q7 Which resources of Z Ltd. do you think are important?

Resources of Z Ltd.	
Human resources (*Hito:* people)	e.g. employees, 2 part-time workers in the future
Material resources (*Mono:* goods)	e.g. PCs, software (the product for sale), tablets, desks, chairs, office space, books, notes, pens
Financial resources (*Kane:* money)	e.g. 2 million yen, 5 million capital, sales and profits
Intellectual resources (*Joho:* information)	e.g. ideas, patents, contents of discussions, brands, customer information

040
Enterprise or company resources are crucial to doing good business. Generally speaking, there are four types of resources: human resources, material resources, financial resources, and intellectual resources. In Japan, it is common to categorize these resources into the following 4 factors: people (*Hito*), goods (*Mono*), money (*Kane*), and information (*Joho*). Considering the Z Ltd. case, you could categorize the resources of Z Ltd. into these 4 factors as in the table above.

Q8 What kinds of things should enterprises or companies think about to best utilize their resources?

041 Enterprise or company resources should be effectively utilized. Companies need to have the ability to combine their resources in order to gain more competitive advantages in the market. This ability is important for each company to survive in a harsh business world, and defines what are often called 'core competencies' for a business. A core competency gives a company a competitive advantage in the market. In other words, it is the ability of a company to use its resources and ingenuity to provide better value to its customers. So what is a concrete example of a core competency? Some examples include technologies or unique products themselves, and others include unique and unmanipulated processes or mechanisms for the business. There are three elements that make up core competencies: (1) added value to the customers; (2) unique competencies that are difficult for other companies to imitate; and (3) the ability to utilize resources in many ways for the company's systems or products.

Q9 Which resource seems most important to you?

042 Resources are limited. You have to think carefully about how to distribute them. Will you use them for a new business or expanding an existing business? One of the most important roles of the president or CEO is making decisions about resource distribution. All four types of resources are important, but some resources are difficult to handle – for example, employees, who are also called human resources. The reason why human resource management (HRM) is difficult is that employers must be concerned with employees' emotions. When you think about HRM, you should not forget that people are commonly working as a team. That is why you have to consider employees not only as a single person but also as a team.

Q10 Do you think HRM is the most important? If so, why? If not, why not?

043 Human resource management (HRM) is a strategic approach that includes the process of recruiting, selecting, and encouraging employees. These are the roles of the human resources (HR) department. The HR department is very important for each company and is responsible for creating, putting into effect, and maintaining policies to govern employees as well as building good relationships between the management team and employees. For instance, when you see a company's recruitment website, there are multiple types of specialized HR positions. Do you understand why these positions are necessary?

Examples of specialist positions in an HR department

Recruiting specialist/manager	Immigration specialist/ manager	Chief Human Resources Officer (CHRO)
Compensation and benefits specialist/manager	Payroll specialist/manager	Talent management specialist/manager
Human resource development specialist/manager	Diversity & inclusion specialist/manager	HR planning specialist/ manager

Task 10 **What interests you most in this article? Write down your ideas.**

コラム❶

コア・コンピタンス (core competence)

　企業における資源は活用されなくては意味がありません。活用するためには、企業がその資源を組み合わせて自社の強みに繋げる能力が必要です。また、それが市場の競争優位 (competitive advantage) につながる必要があります。自社ならではの価値を提供し、それにより顧客がその企業の製品やサービスを選んでくれるという、資源の活用能力のことを、コア・コンピタンスと言います。つまり、顧客に喜ばれる商品やサービスを生み出すために、創意工夫をする力と言えるでしょう。これには、他社にマネされにくい販売の仕組み等も含まれます。コア・コンピタンスの条件は、①顧客の利益につながること ②他社にマネされにくいこと　③それを使ってビジネスや製品が発展可能なことの3つです。

4. Useful words and phrases for business

Task 11 Listen and do shadowing

044

words & phrases	sample sentences
distribute 分配する	The organization **distributed** food to poor people.
e-commerce e コマース	We need to move from traditional business to **e-commerce**.
decision-making 意思決定	The CEO's prompt **decision-making** saved our business.
fiscal year 会計年度	Our business reported a loss in the current **fiscal year**.
enterprise 企業	Make sure to keep in mind that this is a commercial **enterprise**.
found 創設する	She left a huge amount of money in her will to **found** an association for poor people.
accumulate 積み重ねる	The company said that debt had **accumulated**.
patent 特許	The company took out a **patent** on genetically modified food.
allocate 割り当てる	The local government is **allocating** 10 million yen for the project.
limit 制限する	We set a time **limit** of 30 minutes for this meeting.
expand 拡大する	In my opinion, we shouldn't **expand** our business now.
handle 取り扱う	Who **handles** the advertising in your company?
human resource management 人的資源管理	**Human resource management** plays an important role in running a company.

Task 12 For more details, check an online English–English dictionary

1. Use a smartphone or the Internet
2. Select an online English-English dictionary
3. Look up the word(s)
4. Check the results and share ideas with your classmates

5. Research project and discussion

Task 13 **Find interesting crowdfunding in groups**

Have you heard of 'crowdfunding'? It is a system of raising funds with the use of the Internet and social media to collect a small amount of money from a large number of individuals when starting a new business or a project. Try to find some interesting crowdfunding on the Internet and discuss the features of each project.

Your interesting crowdfunding

Name of the project: _____

Aim: _____

Target price: _____

Return: _____

Features: _____

Your classmate's crowdfunding

Name of the project: _____

Aim: _____

Target price: _____

Return: _____

Features: _____

Task 14 **Make a presentation about your interesting crowdfunding**

Which presentation is most impressive?

コラム ②

クラウドファンディング（crowdfunding）

　ヒト、モノ、カネ、情報の４つの経営資源はすべて重要ですが、特にビジネスの初期段階（スタートアップ期）においては、カネを得ること（資金調達）はもっとも頭を悩ませることの一つでしょう。例えば、銀行から資金を借りる場合、銀行はそのビジネスの発展可能性だけでなく、確実に儲かるのか、融資した資金の返済の見込みなどを厳しく審査します。資金調達にはときに確実性や信頼性が求められ、それが資金調達を難しくするのです。そこで、近年、注目を集めるのがクラウドファンディングです。クラウド（crowd：群衆）という言葉からわかるように、インターネット等でビジネスアイデアを伝え、比較的少額の資金を多くの人から集め大きな資金とします。ビジネスの成功時には、出資額に見合ったリターンを渡すと約束し、それに興味を持ち投資をしてくれる人を募るのです。近年、クラウドファンディングは、社会が起業を後押しする有効な方法として注目を集めています。

Chapter 6

Team management

チームのマネジメント

Warmup

Task 1 **Share ideas in English and Japanese**

The various employees who work at a company are its most important resource.
In fact, in business, they are often called human resources. Many activities at the
workplace are strongly related to employees' motivation, so good communication
between colleagues is essential.

Q1 What makes people stay motivated at the workplace?

Q2 The most important factor related to motivation is communication with
colleagues. Do you agree or disagree?

各企業は、「ヒト・モノ・カネ・情報（people, goods, money, information）」という経営
の資源（resources）とその管理（resource management）」に目を向け、それら資源を活用
し、他社に真似されにくい「コア・コンピタンス（core competence）」をいかに作り上げて
いくかを考えます。そして市場での競争優位や、ミッションの達成を目指します。４つの経営
資源の１つである「ヒト」のマネジメントでは、様々な要素を考える必要があります。これに
は、社員のモチベーションや、リーダーシップ、チームワークなどが含まれます。

1. Familiarize yourself with business words and phrases

Motivation is your will to do something proactively. It is said that people's motivation increases more from appreciation, recognition, and challenging opportunities than from an offer of a better salary. Have you had such kinds of experiences in your life?

Task 2 Brainstorm with your classmates

What keeps you motivated when you are working together with other people at a part-time job, in your school's sports team, or for a group assignment?

e.g. I think I am motivated when I am respected by colleagues. Good relationships with others motivate me to do a group assignment.

Task 3 Match each word with the definition

1. motivate (*v.*)
2. human resources (*n.*)
3. wages (*n.*)
4. colleagues (*n.*)
5. workplace (*n.*)

a. people in the same company or organization
b. people who are employed and considered useful assets to a company
c. a building or room where people work
d. to make people want to do something
e. money paid by an employer to a worker for his/ her labor

Task 4 Ask each other

e.g. A: What does 'colleague' mean?
B: It means …

Task 5 Send a message on social media using the above words

e.g. I was very motivated after watching that movie.

2. Preview — The roles of a leader

045

Task 6 Listen and read

There are two main roles as a business leader. One is to share visions and goals with colleagues. The other is to encourage their effectiveness and productivity. It may sound easy, but there are a lot of difficulties in doing so. People are frequently demotivated if they are forced to do something at work. However, people are often motivated when they are delegated the authority to decide things themselves. But on the other hand, if they don't have enough knowledge and skills to do those tasks, they may fail in the end. Every business needs a good leader who can motivate other people and achieve business goals in appropriate ways.

Q3 Do you think you would be a good leader? Are there any good leaders around you?

046

Task 7 Listen and fill in the blanks

Koji (K): Hi, Risa! How are you doing?

Risa (R): Oh, hi, Koji. I've been so busy these days. I'm taking a (1.   ) training course at work for my (2.   ).

K: Sounds great! What kind of training is it? Have you learned anything new about leadership?

R: (3.   ). To be a great leader, first, I must understand my own motivation. After that, I need to (4.   ) open communication in our team so that people can (5.   ) freely.

K: That's interesting. I totally agree that good leadership is a key (6.   ) for a satisfactory project (7.   ).

R: If a leader communicates well, any project will be successful. Learning about leadership has been a great experience for me!

Task 8 Share your thoughts in pairs

Q4 What is ideal leadership for you? What do you think is necessary to be a great leader?

e.g. I think taking full responsibility for the project is necessary.

Q5 What should you do to build a good relationship with your team members?

e.g. I should try to listen to their opinions as much as possible.

3. Topics — People's motivation and team effectiveness

Task 9 Read and discuss each question with your classmates

047 When you work on a team, the leader of the team takes a lot of important roles such as sharing the goal with team members, planning the process to achieve the goal, delegating power and resources to them, and keeping them motivated. Those are the key leadership roles to team effectiveness. In order to further enhance effectiveness, what are other factors that can motivate people?

Q6 What is the theory of human motivation? Do you agree with it?

048 According to Abraham Maslow (1943), a well-known American psychologist, people have 5 kinds of needs. In his theory, people need to be satisfied with these needs in a designated order. It is necessary for people to fulfill their previous needs to move on to the next stage. The first group of needs is located at the bottom of the triangle, and it contains needs related to bodily functions, such as eating, drinking, and sleeping. Once people are satisfied with those needs, they can try to fulfill the next needs – to be safe and secure. After people's security is guaranteed, then they can start to fulfill

their social needs – they would like to have love and belongingness. What do people want next after they meet these social needs? People start to feel the necessity of approval and respect – people's esteem needs. The last and the top human need that Maslow described is self-actualization. It is the only thing that human beings have, but other animals don't.

Maslow believed that people have this hierarchy of needs: physiological, safety, love and belongingness (social), esteem, and self-actualization needs. Business leaders who agree with Maslow's ideas try to increase their colleagues' motivation by giving them opportunities to meet their needs at all levels. Maslow's theory is also useful to help them understand that it is difficult to motivate their colleagues if they are not able to have their most basic needs met.

*Maslow, A. H. (1943). A theory of human motivation. *Psychological Review*, 50(4), 370–396.

Q7 Do you understand Herzberg's two-factor theory? What makes people motivated at the workplace?

 049 Do you think money is the most important thing to keep people motivated? According to Frederick Herzberg's two-factor theory (1959), factors such as a good office location, fair wages, a beautiful and comfortable work environment, and good company policies are called hygiene factors. They need to be provided to avoid employee's dissatisfaction at the workplace. Hygiene factors

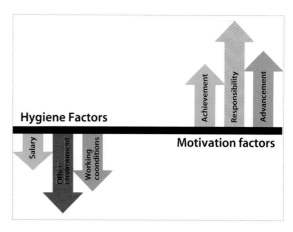

won't lead to additional satisfaction or motivation, however, if they are not fulfilled, people will feel dissatisfaction. There are also other factors called motivation factors (motivators), such as recognition, interest in the work itself, work achievement, and responsibility. These two types of factors are strongly connected to job satisfaction and high motivation.

Think about your part-time job situation, for example. When your hourly wage goes up, you might feel happy and become very motivated at that time. However, one month later, you will forget about this pay raise, and your current wage raised just a month ago will become the new standard for yourself. On the other hand, if you are newly appointed to be a manager, you will feel that you are growing professionally and get more responsibility at work. In this situation, you are more likely to keep your high motivation to fulfill your new role.

*Herzberg, F., Mausner, B., & Snyderman, B. B. (1959). *The Motivation to Work* (2nd ed.). John Wiley & Sons.

Q8 Can you become a good leader? How can you make a team more effective as a leader?

 050 Teamwork is usually important. Working together can save time and provide us with more energy to focus on doing the job. In business, team effectiveness, which refers to the ability to work with other people to accomplish goals or objectives, is important. When a team is created, it usually has a leader. As previously mentioned, motivating team members or followers is one of the most important roles of team leaders. As you understand Herzberg's two-factor theory, you can realize how important it is for employees to be empowered appropriately, have their work recognized, and feel that they contributed. Creating this kind of environment with a good atmosphere at the workplace is key to good teamwork and team effectiveness.

Q9   What is important to be a true leader? What type of leader do you trust?

🎧
051
It is also important for a leader to be trusted by followers. For example, if someone in your work team says, "I have knowledge and skills, so I am qualified as a leader," do you really think this person is the team leader? Would it be okay if the leader was not respected or trusted by followers?

From this example, you can understand that 'leader' and 'leadership' mean different things. The leader is the person who has leadership, while leadership is a characteristic that people want to follow. Leadership may not be able to exist without trust. It is highly important to be a true leader and build credibility among the team members you would like to lead. By doing this, you can take a leadership role in a time of uncertain changes or crisis. If there is trust between the leader and the followers, the followers will think "Let's follow this person!"

Task 10   **What interests you most in this article? Write down your ideas.**

コラム❶   **モチベーションはどこからやってくるか**

　モチベーション（やる気）は自身の欲求と大きく関わります。欲求が行動に移るには、誘因するものが必要です。スイーツを例にとってみると、甘いものが好きな人は「食べたい」という欲求が湧き、「食べる」という行動に移りますが、嫌いな人は食べようとしないでしょう。欲求と誘因が関連して初めて人は行動します。マクレランド（1987）によると、仕事につながる人間の欲求には3つあります。1つめは達成欲求です。何かを達成するために努力したいと内面から湧き出る欲求です。2つめは親和欲求です。職場で楽しく友好的な人間関係を構築したい、自分もその一員でいたいという欲求です。3つめは権力欲求です。誰かの上位に立って影響力を及ぼしたいという欲求です。この中で特に重視されるのは達成欲求です。他の2つは環境的な要因ですが、達成欲求は人間の内部から湧き出る欲求です。働く人々の達成欲求を高めることは、人材のマネジメントで一番難しく重要な部分と言えるでしょう。

4. Useful words and phrases for business

052 **Task 11** Listen and do shadowing

words & phrases	sample sentences
demotivate やる気を失わせる	Setting too high a target is likely to **demotivate** employees.
force 強いて〜させる	The manager **forced** her colleagues to follow her decision.
delegate （権限などを）付与する	The leader should learn to **delegate** tasks to the team members.
outcome(s) 結果、成果	The **outcomes** of this project saved our company.
straightforwardly あからさまに、率直に	My boss told me to express my vision **straightforwardly**.
enhance 高める	It was a good opportunity to **enhance** our company's reputation.
fulfill 果たす、満たす	That candidate **fulfills** all the conditions for employment.
social being 社会的存在	Human beings are **social beings** by nature.
approve 賛成する、よいと認める	The board of directors **approved** the budget.
esteem needs 承認欲求	Getting a promotion is a good way to fulfill your **esteem needs**.
self-actualization 自己実現	**Self-actualization** is the highest human needs.
hygiene factor 衛生要因	**Hygiene factors** include a nice, beautiful, and comfortable office.
recognition 認識、認めること	There's a growing **recognition** that our business is a social good.
empower 権限を与える	The right to vote has **empowered** women.
vital きわめて重要な	The decision to continue this project is **vital** for us.

Task 12 For more details, check an online English-English dictionary

1. Use a smartphone or the Internet
2. Select an online English-English dictionary
3. Look up the word(s)
4. Check the results and share ideas with your classmates

5. Research project and discussion

Task 13 **Do research on entrepreneurs or business leaders in groups**

An entrepreneur is a person who starts a new business with many risks and rewards. The process of starting such a business is called entrepreneurship. Entrepreneurs play a key role in any business, using their knowledge and skills and bringing good new ideas to market.

Which entrepreneur interests you most? Choose one entrepreneur of a start-up or small business venture and search for them on the Internet. You can choose one of the following entrepreneurs if needed.

写真左から　エチオピアでバッグなど革製品を作る㈱andu amet 鮫島弘子さん、
　　　　　　鯖の陸上養殖に挑戦するフィッシュ・バイオテック㈱右田孝宣さん、
　　　　　　広告・プロモーション戦略や動画・イベント等メディアコンテンツを制作する㈱ゴエンジン奥田良太さん、
　　　　　　「実生ゆず」の力で新しいビジネスにチャレンジする「ゆらぎスタイル」㈲re・make 岡山栄子さん

Task 14 **Make a presentation about your favorite entrepreneur in groups**

Which presentation is most impressive?

コラム ❷

リーダーの重要な役割

　　多くのリーダーは、職場の業績に責任を持ちます。また業務を管理・監督をすることも重要な役割の1つです。加えて、部下やチームメンバーの信頼を得ながら、みなの意欲を高め、業績達成に導く役割も担っています。では、リーダーはどのようにこれら2つの役割を遂行しているのでしょうか?まずリーダーは、企業や部門の目標と、部下1人1人の役割をしっかり伝えなくてはなりません。そして部下の仕事ぶりや進捗を監督することも重要です。コラム①でも説明した通り、目標や役割を、部下の欲求に関連づけてしっかり伝えることは、部下のモチベーションを高めます。しかし、実際にはリーダーが仕事の監督だけを行っている場合も多く、管理監督が行き過ぎると、逆に部下の「やる気」を削ぐ結果になります。みなさんが職場でリーダーを任されたときには、目標共有や、部下への動機付けをしっかり遂行できることが期待されているのです。

Chapter 7

The Japanese HRM system

日本型人事管理

Warmup

Task 1 **Share ideas in English and Japanese**

It is critical for all companies to hire employees and manage them as human resources. This is called Human Resource Management (HRM). HRM includes setting in-house rules and regulations, evaluation systems, compensation, and benefits. Having excellent HRM is a great incentive for people to apply to join a company.

Q1 What are the functions of the HR department?

Q2 What is a great incentive for you to join a company?

組織には多くの社員がおり、規程や制度で全体をコントロールすることが必要です。この企業内の「ヒトを管理する仕組み（人事管理：human resource management ― HRM）」に焦点を当ててみましょう。多くの日本企業では、「新卒一括採用・長期雇用・年功賃金制度」という、社会システムとも密接につながった人事管理が行われています。本章では、多くの企業で取り入れられている「目標による管理（management by objectives: MBO）」制度や、世界で見ても特殊な日本の「新卒採用（hiring of new college graduates）」に触れていきます。

1. Familiarize yourself with business words and phrases

To start working at a company, you first need to submit a resume or job application. If you join the company as a full-time worker, you can get compensation and benefits such as medical insurance and pension. You will sometimes get more, such as support for rent, the use of company-owned resorts, paid holidays, and nursery support.

Task 2 Brainstorm with your classmates

What kind of things do you need to write in your resume when you apply for a company? What employee benefits do you expect from your company, in particular?

e.g. I need to write my academic achievements and work experience.
I'd like to have a lot of paid holidays because I want to enjoy my life.

Task 3 Match each word with the definition

1. personality (*n.*)
2. drive (*v.*)
3. fringe benefits (*n.*)
4. incentive (*n.*)
5. applicant (*n.*)

a. economic benefits that a company provides to its employees in addition to their salaries
b. something that is given externally as encouragement
c. a person who formally requests a job
d. a person's character as an independent individual
e. to force someone to act in some way or another

Task 4 Ask each other

e.g. A: What does 'drive' mean?
B: It means ...

Task 5 Send a message on social media using the above words

e.g. This company provides excellent fringe benefits to its employees.

2. Preview — Management by objectives (MBO)

Task 6 **Listen and read**

053

There are several systems used to evaluate employees. Many companies use a system called management by objectives (MBO). It is a system in which goals are set for each individual or group. This system was developed for evaluation and the development of employees. The goals should be agreed upon by the supervisors and employees. They should be clear, specific, and not too difficult to achieve. Once the goals are set, it should be decided when to evaluate achievement. MBO is a good process in which the supervisors and employees set goals together and regularly evaluate their achievements.

Q3 Have you heard about MBO before? What do you think about it?

Task 7 **Listen and fill in the blanks**

054

Jun (J): Hi, how was your job interview?

Taka (T): I was very nervous when I visited NK company this morning. It was my first job interview.

J: Did it go okay?

T: It was a group (¹.   ). I don't know if I did better than others, but I learned a lot from other applicants' (².   ). It definitely is useful for my (³.   ) job hunting.

J: Future job hunting? Won't you take NK company's (⁴.   ) if you pass?

T: Yes, NK company is my first choice, but I am not sure if I will pass. Even if I pass, I will (⁵.   ) have to go to two more interviews. So, I am now applying to three other companies.

Task 8 **Share your thoughts in pairs**

Q4 Can you introduce yourself well for a job interview? What's your strong point?

e.g. My name is Tomo Tanaka. I have a lot of friends, and everybody says I am a trustworthy person. I always try to help other people if they need any help.

Q5 Talk about the best experiences or activities in your life.

e.g. I've belonged to the student orchestra since I was in high school. I play violin and I've practiced so hard.

3. Topics – The Japanese human resources management system

Task 9 Read and discuss each question with your classmates

055 The Japanese HRM (human resources management) system is unique. There are three main features of Japanese HRM: lifetime employment, a seniority wage system, and the periodic recruiting of new graduates. They are seldom seen outside Japan; therefore, the Japanese HRM system is truly unique in the world.

Q6 Why do Japanese companies have such a unique HRM system? Do you like it or not?

056 These three features of the Japanese HRM system are deeply linked to each other. Many Japanese companies hire new college graduates at the same time, usually once a year. This is called the periodic recruiting system. This is strongly linked with the lifetime employment system – every year, a group of employees at the retirement age of 60 to 65 leave their companies at the same time. Thus, companies must hire new employees to compensate for those retired people. Based on this cycle, it is assumed that most people will not leave the company until their retirement, so a seniority wage system is indispensable for the company and employees. Newly hired young people can expect stable pay raises until they retire. Although people commonly need more money in their 40's and 50's, they do not need to worry too much about it thanks to this system. This has been the traditional Japanese employment system, but the situation is slowly changing in recent years.

Labor force population and labor force participation rate

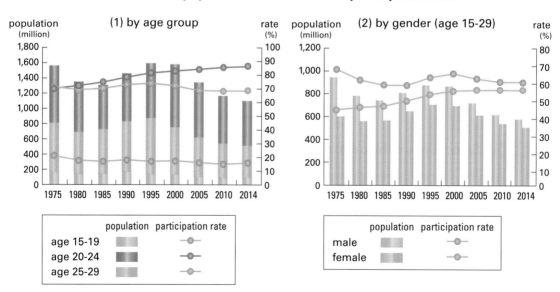

Source: Ministry of General Affairs "Labour Force Survey 2015"
The Labor force population is the sum of all persons 15 years of age or older that are employed or completely unemployed.

Q7 How should the traditional Japanese HRM system or Japanese employment system be changed?

057

The Japanese HRM is developing to meet changes in the environment surrounding our lives such as demographic changes in the Japanese population and globalization. With these changes, companies need to hire more diverse employees like women, foreigners, and seniors. If Japanese companies are too focused on the periodic recruiting of new graduates, it will be increasingly difficult for them to hire new employees as the population of new graduates decreases. Furthermore, due to globalization, there is a larger variety of customers in the market. To satisfy these various customers, companies need to hire more diverse people so that they can understand customers' points of view. As mentioned, lifetime employment, the seniority wage system, and the periodic recruiting of new graduates have been features of many Japanese companies for a long time. The HRM system has been designed with these features in mind. However, due to environmental and market changes that Japanese companies face, they are now trying to develop their HRM systems to meet the new era.

Q8 What kind of abilities and skills do you need to be hired by companies?

058

In 2006, the Ministry of Economy, Trade, and Industry (METI) proposed the concept of "Basic Skills for Working People," which consists of the following three abilities: "the ability to take action," "the ability to think critically," and "the ability to work as a team." These three abilities consist of 12 elements of competence. This concept has become increasingly important under the instability of what is referred to as the era of VUCA.

* The era of VUCA (Volatility · Uncertainty · Complexity · Ambiguity): 既存の価値観やビジネスモデルなどが通用しない時代のこと。

The Concept of "Basic Skills for Working People"

Ability to Take Action

Can move forward and persevere even when facing failure

Can work proactively

Can work with and involve others

Can get things done by setting goals and achieving them

Critical Thinking

Can find issues and think things through

Can analyze situations to clarify objectives and identify issues

Can make plans to solve problems

Can create new value

Teamwork

Can cooperate with diverse people

Can communicate and share opinions clearly

Can actively listen to others' opinions

Can show flexibility and understand differences in opinion and perspective

Ability to understand the current situation, including the relationships between surrounding people and things

Can reliably follow social rules and keep promises to others

Can deal with stress and its causes

経済産業省 (2006)「社会人基礎力」を翻訳・加筆修正の上、作成。https://www.meti.go.jp

[Sample] Basic Skills for Working People Self-evaluation

Self-evaluation   **1**: Not at all   **2**: Yes, moderately   **3**: I'm not sure   **4**: Yes, mostly
                        5: Yes, very much

	Elements to evaluate	Self-evaluation Put the number here	Reason for the score (Concrete examples of past behaviors to evaluate yourself)
Ability to Take Action	Can work proactively		e.g. I planned a charity concert for the school choir and played a key role in negotiating with XX city to collaborate.
	Can work with and involve others		
	Can get things done by setting goals and achieving them		
Critical Thinking	Can analyze situations to clarify objectives and identify issues		e.g. I suggested in my economy class to create a group of staff who support foreign students.
	Can make plans to solve problems		
	Can create new value		
Teamwork	Can communicate and share opinions clearly		e.g. In my freshman class, we decided to open a café at the school festival. At that time, I actively gave opinions on marketing and listened to others. I played a facilitator role in the meeting.
	Can actively listen to others' opinions		
	Can show flexibility and understand differences in opinion and perspective		
	Ability to understand the current situation, including the relationships between surrounding people and things		
	Can reliably follow social rules and keep promises to others		
	Can deal with stress and its causes		

経済産業省 (2006).「社会人基礎力」を基に翻訳・加筆修正の上、作成。https://www.meti.go.jp

Task 10 **What interests you most in this article? Write down your ideas.**

コラム ❶

日本型の採用と人事管理

　新卒一括採用 (the periodic recruiting of new college graduates) は、世界ではまれな採用システムです。日本の企業が新卒一括採用を行う理由を考えてみましょう。現在は労働市場がかなり多様化していますが、多くの日本企業ではいまだ長期的な視点での人事管理 (human resource management: HRM) が主流です。そのため、定年退職者や離職者の数を考慮して新卒者を採用することは、企業には人員計画が立てやすいという利点があります。一方で、企業は経験やスキルのない新卒者に様々な部署で経験を積ませ、長期的に育成する必要がありますが、それにはコストも時間もかかります。そしてこれは、社員がその企業に勤め続けることを前提としているからこそ成り立ちます。なお、社内の役職は限られていることから、長期雇用と育成を行う企業では、昇進・昇格のペースは一般的に緩やかになります。

4. Useful words and phrases for business

Task 11 Listen and do shadowing

059

words & phrases	sample sentences
supervisor 上司	His **supervisor** shows great leadership and care.
applicant 応募者	There were many **applicants** for the full-time position.
emphasize 強調する	The sales promotion **emphasized** the convenience of this service.
compensate 補う	The organizer had to **compensate** for the cancellation of that event.
indispensable 絶対必要な、避けられない	Secure information is **indispensable** at work.
periodic 定期的な	The company should consider the **periodic** change in conditions in its industry.
era 時代	Our company was set up in the *Reiwa* **era**.

Task 12 For more details, check an online English-English dictionary

1. Use a smartphone or the Internet
2. Select an online English-English dictionary
3. Look up the word(s)
4. Check the results and share ideas with your classmates

5. Research project and discussion

Task 13 **Learn about the HRM system in groups**

There are some advantages and disadvantages of the Japanese HRM system, which has some specific features: the lifetime employment system, the seniority wage system, and the periodic recruiting system. Discuss the advantages and disadvantages with your classmates and complete the table. If you could change these systems, how would you improve them?

	advantages	disadvantages
The lifetime employment system		
The seniority wage system		
The periodic recruiting system		

Task 14 **Make a presentation about the HRM system**

Which presentation is most impressive?

コラム ❷

メンバーシップ型 VS ジョブ型

　最近、よく耳にするメンバーシップ型雇用、ジョブ型雇用という言葉を知っていますか？メンバーシップ型雇用は、日本型の人事管理と親和性があります。日本型の人事管理は、新卒一括採用と長期雇用が前提であるとコラム①で述べました。しかし、企業が社員を長期間、雇い続けることは、実は容易なことではありません。多くの場合、「職務を限定しない（企業からの辞令により、幅広い職務を担う）」ことが暗黙の条件となっています。職務を限定せず、企業の一員として様々なことに貢献する―それがメンバーシップ型雇用です。メンバーシップ型では、企業は人材の将来性を見込んで、仕事の経験を通して育成するという面があります。一方で、ジョブ型雇用では、「このポジションには、この職務」とあらかじめ職務の内容が決まっており、その仕事ができる人材を採用します。成果が出れば評価も上がりますが、成果が出せなければシビアな評価が下ります。よって、経験やスキルが不足している新卒学生には不利な面があるとも考えられます。加えて、必要なスキル・経験も、自律的に構築する必要があります。近年、この2つの雇用形態が対比されることが多いですが、両方に長所と短所があるのです。

Chapter 8

What is marketing?

マーケティングとは

Warmup

Task 1 Share ideas in English and Japanese

Marketing is how companies create products and services to meet the customers' needs. A company can decide what kind of products and services it sells to the customers and how it sells them. For example, a department store and a shopping mall sell various products, but they have different types of marketing.

Q1 Which do you prefer to shop at, a department store or a shopping mall?

Q2 What are the differences between a department store and a shopping mall?

マーケティングでは、顧客が望む商品やサービスを把握し、その価格や売る方法を考えます。例えば、カバンを例に考えてみましょう。「誰のための、どんなカバンを、どこで、いくらで、どうやって売るのか」―私たちが普段何気なく購入する商品であっても、これらは企業内でしっかりと考えられています。ここでは、マーケット（市場）とは何か、そしてマーケティング分析の1つの手法であるSTP分析（segmentation, targeting, positioning）について理解を深めます。マーケティングにおける「市場」とは、「この商品・サービスを買いそうな顧客のグループ」を意味します。STP分析では、市場をさらに同類グループに切り分け（segmentation）、そのうちのどこで（targeting）、どんな立ち位置から（positioning）顧客に商品・サービスを提供するのかを考えます。

1. Familiarize yourself with business words and phrases

Product, price, place, and promotion are referred to as the 4 Ps of marketing. The 4 Ps are used by companies when they identify concrete ways to reach customers effectively. The price, place, and promotion should be decided by what kind of products (or services) the company sells and to whom.

PRODUCT   PRICE   PLACE   PROMOTION

Task 2 Brainstorm with your classmates

If you buy a wallet, for example, which store would you go to or what product would you buy? Would you consider the price or advertising for the product?

e.g. I would choose the nearest store and buy the cheapest one. I don't care about the brand, but I would check the price.

Task 3 Match each word with the definition

1. shop (*v.*)
2. luxury (*n.*)
3. wrap (*v.*)
4. security (*n.*)
5. mass-produced (*adj.*)
6. groceries (*n.*)

a. something special and expensive
b. protection against something dangerous
c. produced in large quantities using machines
d. to visit a store to buy something
e. the food and other daily necessities sold at a supermarket
f. to put paper or other material over something to cover it

Task 4 Ask each other

e.g. A: What does 'luxury' mean?
　　　 B: It means …

Task 5 Send a message on social media using the above words

e.g. I would like to shop at many boutiques in Tokyo.

2. Preview — The process of marketing

060

Task 6 **Listen and read**

The basic process of marketing is creating products and services to meet the customers' needs. Marketing activities start with an analysis of the current situation in the market. For example, do the customers accept the products and services that a company sells? How many sales or how much market share does the company currently have? Who are its competitors in the market? What kind of channels does it use

to reach the customers? Based on these analyses, each company considers new plans to create and sell products or services. The important thing is to know who the customers are, what the products or services are, how they are offered, and how the relationships are deepened and maintained. This is called the marketing management process.

Q3 Which step of the marketing management process do you think is most important?

061

Task 7 **Listen and fill in the blanks**

Koji (K): Hey, check it out. I have ($^{1.}$) these newly launched sneakers. I thought I couldn't get them. So exciting!

Risa (R): Oh, good for you. But I don't quite understand why they are so great. How much are they?

K: They cost ($^{2.}$) yen plus tax.

R: Did you really pay that ($^{3.}$) for sneakers? I can't believe it.

K: Listen, they have ($^{4.}$) to me. For me, I really don't understand why people pay a lot of money for ($^{5.}$). The trends in clothes change so quickly, so it's a ($^{6.}$) of money.

R: I usually buy them at fast fashion stores. I don't spend much money buying shoes or clothes. I wonder what the marketing ($^{7.}$) process for sneakers is.

Task 8 **Share your thoughts in pairs**

Q4 Do you buy goods on the Internet? What kind of goods do you prefer to buy through the Internet rather than at real stores?

e.g. I buy clothes at real stores because I can try them on.

Q5 What do you think about the marketing management process for sneakers?

e.g. I think high-price snakers are sold.

3. Topics — Segmentation, targeting, and positioning (STP)

Task 9 Read and discuss each question with your classmates

In order to promote effective marketing, it is necessary to analyze the external and internal environment and set targets for marketing activities. Sales, profits, market presence, and market share are all targets. To create an effective marketing plan, STP should first be considered.

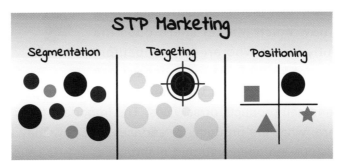

Q6 What is STP marketing? How useful is it?

STP stands for "segmentation, targeting, and positioning." Simply speaking, it describes the 3 marketing phases that companies should do first when preparing marketing activities. The 3 phases consist of creating market segmentation, targeting the selected segments, and setting targets to develop products or services.

By conducting STP as a marketing process, you can find out the 'needs' and 'wants' of customers in the market, define good customers who buy products and services, and then set a firm position in the market to distinguish your company from competitors. Also, STP shows how the benefits are communicated to the customers segmented and targeted. In a nutshell, the STP marketing model is useful in creating a successful marketing strategy.

Q7 Why does a company need to do STP marketing?

The first step for STP marketing is to segment the market into some specific groups. Then, you decide on customer groups to target for the products or services of your company. Finally, carefully set the position of products and services in the market from the view of differentiation from competitors, according to potential customers' expectations and needs. To make good use of the STP model, a company has to understand what the market shows. The company is required to keep in mind that people have a variety of values and interests. In the market, there are various customers' 'needs' and 'wants.' It is difficult for companies to meet all of these, so a company segments the market into groups of people who have similar 'needs' or 'wants.' Using demographic and geographic points of view for segmentation is the common and popular way. Then, the company decides on target customers from the segmented groups. This makes it easier for companies to develop specific products or services. After deciding on the group of target customers, companies have to think about how to differentiate from other companies' products or services to build a position in the market. This is the process of STP marketing.

Q8 What is segmentation? How do you do segmentation in the marketing process?

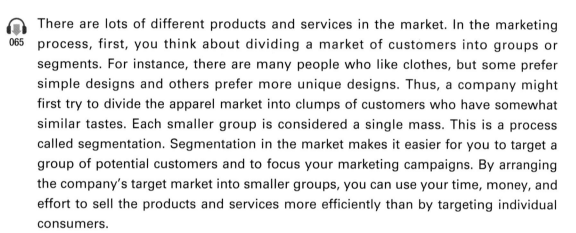

065 There are lots of different products and services in the market. In the marketing process, first, you think about dividing a market of customers into groups or segments. For instance, there are many people who like clothes, but some prefer simple designs and others prefer more unique designs. Thus, a company might first try to divide the apparel market into clumps of customers who have somewhat similar tastes. Each smaller group is considered a single mass. This is a process called segmentation. Segmentation in the market makes it easier for you to target a group of potential customers and to focus your marketing campaigns. By arranging the company's target market into smaller groups, you can use your time, money, and effort to sell the products and services more efficiently than by targeting individual consumers.

Q9 What is targeting? How do you do targeting in the marketing process?

066 Even among those segmented customers who like simple clothes, some may like the color red, and others may like the color blue. All people have different characteristics in some way, so it is impossible to meet everyone's needs. Even if a company tries to satisfy all the customers in all segmented groups, it is very difficult to do so. In management, you have to make a profit. Thus, after dividing the market into some segmented groups, a company will need to decide which groups to target and develop products or services for them. This is called targeting.

Q10 What is positioning? How do you do positioning in the marketing process?

067

Positioning is the process of differentiating the products (or services) from others for targeted customers in the market. In other words, it is the process of getting the customers or potential customers to recognize that only certain specific products or services can satisfy their particular needs. It is necessary for a company to show the unique value that will be provided by the products or services. This unique added value is critical to establishing the concept of the product, which is very important in marketing. If a company offers a product or service with a clear concept, it will be easier for the company to decide how it will sell the product or service to target customers.

For example, if you are a customer and you want to buy a suitcase, what kind of suitcase would you like to buy? If you are an elderly person, lightness might be very important. If you go on business trips frequently, durability might be the most important feature. To reach the target customers, a product's image must be clearly conveyed in the market. This is what the company has to do for positioning.

Task 10 **What interests you most in this article? Write down your ideas.**

コラム❶
セグメンテーション（segmentation）の難しさ

　セグメンテーション—市場を切り分けるという点について考えてみましょう。マーケティングを行うにあたって、市場のすべてを対象にすると、あまりにもコストがかかりすぎます。企業の資源は有限なので、それを市場での競争において、どう有効に使うかを決める必要があります。例えばスーツケースとリュックでは、製品の材料や製造方法、用途、顧客、ニーズ、販売する場所などがまったく異なります。市場のニーズに対応し、効率よく製造・販売するために、カバン市場を「スーツケースの市場」や「リュックの市場」に切り分けます。さらにリュックであれば、「学校用リュック」「登山用のリュック」等に切り分け可能です。それにより「どんな材料を使用するか」「どこで売るか」が考えやすくなります。なお、この時、注意が必要なのは、「もれなくダブりなく（MECE）」で切り分けることです。それにより、切り分けた市場での顧客ニーズがより明確になります。
※MECE: Mutually Exclusive, Collectively Exhaustive の略

4. Useful words and phrases for business

Task 11 **Listen and do shadowing**

words & phrases	sample sentences
fluctuating 変動する	With this trade, there is a risk of **fluctuating** exchange rates.
skyrocket 急上昇する	The price of oil was **skyrocketing** due to the oil crisis.
segmentation 分割	Market **segmentation** is an important part of marketing.
presence 存在	The American **presence** in Okinawa is a big issue.
distribution 流通	The **distribution** industry was limited during the Olympic Games.
positioning （存在している）位置	Understanding your **positioning** is a shortcut to getting promoted.
manufacture 製造	It is the biggest company in the steel **manufacturing** industry.
potential 可能性	That start-up has huge **potential**.
preference 好み	This product suits the **preferences** of the Asian market.
perception 認識	We have to change the customer's **perception** for sustainability.
lightness 軽いこと	The main advantage of this product is its **lightness**.
durability 耐久性	This watch has a good reputation for its **durability**.
convey 伝える、伝達する	She always **conveys** a sense of enthusiasm for her work.

Task 12 **For more details, check an online English-English dictionary**

1. Use a smartphone or the Internet
2. Select an online English-English dictionary
3. Look up the word(s)
4. Check the results and share ideas with your classmates

5. Research project and discussion

Task 13 **Conduct an STP analysis in groups**

Choose one company in any industry and describe its marketing strategies which cover its segmentation, targeting, and positioning.

Company's name	
Industry	
Segmentation of the company in the industry	
Targeting of potential customers	
Positioning of the company in the industry	

Task 14 **Make a presentation about the STP marketing model**

Which presentation is most impressive?

コラム **❷**

ターゲティング（targeting）とポジショニング（positioning）

　セグメンテーションが終わると、切り分けた市場の中からどの市場に資源を投入するかを考えます。これをターゲティング（targeting）と言います。ターゲティングを行うには、その市場の成長見込みや顧客ニーズの測定可能性、またそれらの顧客に自社の資源でリーチできるか、という見極めが重要になります。例えば、カバン市場における「ランドセルに代わる小学生用のリュック」の市場が成長しそうで、ニーズが見込めるとしても、販売拠点の開拓ができない場合、市場への参入は難しいでしょう。

　もし、「ランドセルに代わる小学生用のリュック」市場に見込みがあり、参入を検討する場合は、すでに先を行く競合他社の存在を前提に、同じ市場で「どういった立ち位置を自分たちが取るか」を考える必要があります。これをポジショニング（positioning）と言います。たとえば、自社のカバンは「品質と素材の良さ」が認められており、他社と差別化ができる場合、「小学生用のスクール・リュック」も「品質と素材の良さ」で勝負し、市場でポジションを得るという選択があるでしょう。

Chapter 9

The marketing mix

マーケティング・ミックス

Warmup

Task 1 **Share ideas in English and Japanese**

A marketing mix consists of four elements: product, price, place, and promotion. A company sells products or services, and the price is determined by how much the company expects customers to pay for them. Place decisions can directly affect the company's promotion activities. The marketing mix is essential for successful marketing.

Q1 You might often buy snacks. What kind of snacks do you like to eat? Choose a snack and think about the price, the place where it is sold, and the promotion.

Q2 E-commerce is becoming popular. What kind of products do you buy on the Internet? What do you think about the marketing mix for these products?

> STP 分析により参入し、競争する市場が決まった後にはマーケティングの「4つの P」が重要となります。「4つの P」とは、売る製品（Product）・価格（Price）・販売チャネル（Place）・製品のプロモーション（Promotion）です。みなさんが普段買っているお菓子はどんな製品で価格はいくらでしょうか？また、人々はどうやってその商品を知るのでしょう？企業は、自社の製品について、ターゲットとなる顧客のニーズに合致した価格、販売経路、プロモーションを考えます。ここでは「マーケティングの 4P」について、より深く学びましょう。

1. Familiarize yourself with business words and phrases

There is a variety of chocolate you can buy at the store. Let's think about the marketing mix of chocolate using the 4Ps:

· Product or service: design, quality, features, packaging, etc.
· Price: brand, concept of products, discounts, etc.
· Place: distribution, target customers, the eye of the consumer, etc.
· Promotion: advertising, public relations, word of mouth, press reports, incentives, etc.

Task 2 Brainstorm with your classmates

Choose one brand of chocolate. Share the product name, its price, promotion, and place with your classmates.

e.g. We chose XX. It is a very famous brand. The price is very high and it is sold all over the world. Many people want to buy and eat it.

Task 3 Match each word with the definition

1. element (*n.*)
2. channel (*n.*)
3. refer (*v.*)
4. interaction (*n.*)
5. nowadays (*adv.*)

a. an occasion in which people communicate
b. recently, these days
c. to mention or cite
d. a basic part of something
e. a way of making a product available

Task 4 Ask each other

e.g. A: What does 'interaction' mean?
      B: It means ...

Task 5 Send a message on social media using the above words

e.g. Our teacher said she will refer to this topic in the next class.

2. Preview — The marketing mix

Task 6 **Listen and read**
069

Food products rich in protein are very popular. Consumers are becoming more health-conscious, recognizing protein is important for building muscle and maintaining good health. "Salad-chicken" is already known as a dish with high protein. However, food companies have recently

写真提供：日本ルナ株式会社
写真は2022年時点のものです

started to produce a variety of high-protein products. For example, Nippon Luna Ltd., a group of NH Foods Ltd., manufactures and sells a fat free dairy product which contains about two or three times more protein than ordinary yogurt. Other companies are also developing high protein products, such as a pasta product that contains 60% more protein than ordinary pastas. Another company sells a soup product that has seven times more protein than regular corn cream soup. Food companies believe that there are still many consumers who want to get more protein from daily dishes.

Q3   Do you want to eat food rich in protein? What kind of high-protein foods have you eaten?

Task 7 **Listen and fill in the blanks**
070

Risa (R): What flyer are you reading? A new furniture (¹.   ) store?

Koji (K): Yeah. It says a huge furniture store with foreign (².   ) will open in Kyoto next month.

R: How cool! I love that furniture brand. Its furniture is simple and well-designed. The price is (³.   ), isn't it?

K: Yes, I think so. I am planning to move to a new apartment, so it is great news. The problem is, I don't have a car. The store will be (⁴.   ) in the suburbs, and it doesn't have a delivery service. This is a big (⁵.   ) for me.

R: Well, that store has an e-commerce website as another (⁶.   ) channel, right?

K: That's right. That furniture company does have an online store. Thanks.

Task 8 **Share your thoughts in pairs**

Q4   Every year there are a lot of new products. What is the most impressive new product to you? Why?

e.g.   I am really impressed with a new laundry detergent. It is in the shape of a cube. It is very cute and effective.

Q5   What is the most expensive product you bought last year? Why did you buy it?

e.g.   I bought a chair at an online store because it was quicker and more convenient.

3. Topics — The marketing mix — A case study: Pocky chocolate and Bâton d'or

Task 9 **Read and discuss each question with your classmates**

071

Have you heard of a Japanese sweet snack named "Bâton d'or," a high-end version of Pocky chocolate produced by Ezaki Glico Co., Ltd.? Pocky chocolate has been also sold by that company since the 1960s. Although Bâton d'or is based on the idea of Pocky chocolate, which has been very familiar to many since childhood, the Bâton d'or series has become very popular as a gift or souvenir in the several years since its release. The case of Bâton d'or is helpful to understand the marketing mix: product, price, place, and promotion.

写真提供：江崎グリコ株式会社

Q6 What do you think about Glico's marketing for Pocky chocalate and Bâton d'or?

072

Pocky chocolate is the brand name of a Japanese popular snack you will see at most supermarkets and convenience stores. Each snack is shaped like a thin biscuit or pretzel stick, partly coated with chocolate. One end of each stick is uncoated so that you can hold it easily with your fingers. Because of not only its unique and well-considered shape but also its good taste, Pocky chocolate has been a popular long-selling product since it made its debut in Japan in 1966. In addition, the price is very reasonable. One pack costs about 170 yen and contains two plastic bags of snacks. These snacks are therefore very popular in many countries now.

Q7 Do you know the brand name Bâton d'or? Where can you buy it?

073

Pocky chocolate and Bâton d'or have a similar shape, but each stick of Bâton d'or is thicker than that of Pocky chocolate. Bâton d'or sticks contain more butter than Pocky chocolate. When Ezaki Glico Co.,Ltd. developed Bâton d'or, the amount of high-quality butter and sugar as ingredients was considered very carefully. This unique recipe gives Bâton d'or a very nice aroma. Bâton d'or is specifically targeted at adults and introduced several grown-up biscuit or pretzel stick snacks. Pocky chocolate is sold to families at supermarkets and convenience stores, while Bâton d'or is sold at department stores as a gift or souvenir. At first, Bâton d'or was only available at two

写真提供：江崎グリコ株式会社
商品パッケージは変更の可能性があります。

department stores in Osaka. Before it was launched, many people were suspicious of its sale at department stores, probably because Pocky chocolate had an inexpensive image among people. However, Bâton d'or became such a luxury image with the reputation of good taste that many customers waited in long lines to buy it before the department stores opened. The prices of the Bâton d'or series are now around 600 yen or more per box, more than three times the price of Pocky chocolate. Due to its popularity, Bâton d'or soon started to be sold in Kyoto and Fukuoka as well. Since the year 2017, the Bâton d'or series has started to expand its channels to sell in some department stores around Japan, some airports, and online.

Q8 What do you think about the packaging design? After reading this example, check some package designs around you.

074

As you see, the packaging design in the Bâton d'or series looks very luxurious. Their packages are truly suitable for gifts or souvenirs. In addition, the sales staff wear stylish uniforms, and there are various flavors of Bâton d'or being sold. Seasonal and limited flavors are also promoted sometimes, and are very popular. Because chocolate is difficult to handle in the hot summertime, biscuit or pretzel sticks with no chocolate coating are also developed and sold.

Q9 What do you think about this case study of Pocky chocolate and Bâton d'or?

075

写真提供：江崎グリコ株式会社

Through this case study, you can hopefully understand the importance of the 4Ps marketing mix: product, price, place, and promotion. After identifying target customers with STP, each company starts to think about a concrete way to reach and attract those target customers. To make a suitable marketing strategy for those targeted customers, considering the marketing mix consisting of 4Ps (product, price, place, promotion) is a very important process. Arranging these elements of the marketing mix and making profitable marketing decisions at every level is the key to expanding the sales of a company. The marketing mix, an important set of marketing tools, helps companies make decisions and create unique strategies for a new business in the market, as shown in this case study.

※価格等は 2022 年 11 月時点のものである。

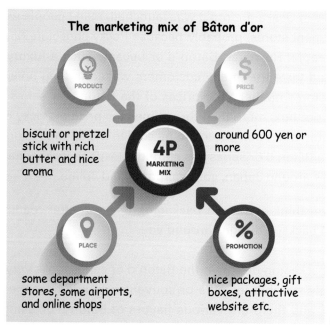

The marketing mix of Bâton d'or

PRODUCT
biscuit or pretzel stick with rich butter and nice aroma

PRICE
around 600 yen or more

4P MARKETING MIX

PLACE
some department stores, some airports, and online shops

PROMOTION
nice packages, gift boxes, attractive website etc.

※著者による分析

Task 10 What interests you most in this article? Write down your ideas.

コラム❶

マーケティングの4P

　STP分析が良いものであれば、マーケティングの4Pは考えやすくなります。「ランドセルに代わる小学生用のリュック」の例を再び振り返りましょう。まず、この製品のターゲット顧客は、小学生と親（購入者）です。Product（製品）の観点からは、革のランドセルが満たせてないニーズを考えます。例えば、素材の扱いやすさ、重さはどうでしょう。また、リュックを使ってみたい小学生は、ランドセルは個性がないと考えているかもしれません。Price（価格）は、革以外を使うなら下がるでしょう。価格はリュックの大きな差別化ポイントになりそうです。Place（販売チャネル）は、親子で買いに来るなら、デパートやショッピングモールが良さそうです。Promotion（販売促進）は、例えば、限定品のキャラクター付き商品も販売し、そのキャラクターが出る番組の間にCMを流すのはどうでしょうか。このように、STPをしっかり考えると、4Pがぐっと考えやすくなります。

4. Useful words and phrases for business

076

Task 11 **Listen and do shadowing**

words & phrases	sample sentences
health-conscious 健康志向の	There are many **health-conscious** people in this area.
intake 摂取	Researchers investigated the **intake** of air in the water pipe.
ordinary 普通の	**Ordinary** people don't like to buy expensive products.
flyer チラシ	The owner ordered a thousand **flyers** yesterday.
high-end 最高仕様の	The brand launched a **high-end** product to attract celebrities.
reasonable 適正の	The prices are quite **reasonable** at the newly opened restaurant.
available 利用可能な	Are there any rooms **available** during the New Year's holidays?
suspicious 疑わしい	Employees are **suspicious** of the sales.
luxurious 豪華な、贅沢な	We'd like to stay in a **luxurious** hotel someday.
refrigeration 冷蔵	A **refrigeration** system is necessary to keep foods fresh.

Task 12 **For more details, check an online English–English dictionary**

1. Use a smartphone or the Internet
2. Select an online English-English dictionary
3. Look up the word(s)
4. Check the results and share ideas with your classmates

5. Research project and discussion

Task 13 **Do research on the marketing mix in groups**

Select a product and do research on the 4Ps of the marketing mix: product, price, place, and promotion. Then, make a POP advertisement to promote a new product or service in groups.

*POP (point of purchase) advertising: Promotion pop-ups at the store

Task 14 **Make a presentation about the marketing mix**

Which presentation is most impressive?

コラム ❷

お菓子の「おとな味」

　コンビニでもよく「大人の…」といったフレーズのお菓子や食べ物を見かけます。4P の視点で見ると、Product（製品）のターゲットを子供から大人に変えることで、Price（価格）は高く設定できそうだということがわかるでしょうか。恐らく、これらの「おとな味」は、CM や販売促進の方法も違っているはずです。ぜひ、インターネットやお店でチェックしてみてください。なお、マーケティングとは様々なデータや資料から分析を行った上で、まだ可視化されていないニーズを汲み取り、市場を開拓していくものです。このようなマーケティングの専門家を「マーケター」と言います。ち密な分析力と、創造性の両方が必要な仕事と言えるでしょう。

Warmup

Task 1 | Share ideas in English and Japanese

Companies sell products or services to customers and customers buy them. This generates 'sales' – a business word for income. However, if companies also spend money to prepare these products or services, it is called 'cost.' When you run your own business, you need to have a good grasp of the financial status of your business.

Q1   What kinds of costs do you think are necessary to run a café?

Q2   How would you raise the capital to open a new café? What are the names of documents for tracking financial status related to your business?

> どんなに優れた商品やサービスのアイデアがあっても、「カネ」がなければ企業は動くことができません。そこで、資金調達のために、企業の多くは株式発行やクラウドファンディングで投資を集めたり、金融機関から借入を行います。その際、投資家や銀行の大きな判断材料になるものが、財務諸表です。財務諸表は企業の通信簿のようなもので、企業が利益を出しているか、健全な経営をしているかなど、多くのことがこれらの書類から見えてきます。

1. Familiarize yourself with business words and phrases

It is important to carefully watch the financial status of a company. From the financial statements, not only business owners but also banks and investors can see how well the business is being operated. Profit and loss (P&L) statements, balance sheets, and cash flow statements are key to checking a company's performance.

FINANCIAL STATEMENT

Task 2 Brainstorm with your classmates

Categorize the financial phrases below into two different groups: either a company's money 'inflow' or 'outflow.'

1. wages for employees   2. rent for the office   3. money from investors
4. borrowed money from a bank   5. payment for materials
6. supporting funds for cultural events   7. money collected by crowdfunding
8. welfare expenses for employees   9. payment from customers when purchasing products
10. memberships fees from customers for services provided

money inflow	money outflow

Task 3 Match each word with the definition

1. flow (*n.*)
2. cost (*n.*)
3. have a grasp of (*v.*)
4. financial (*adj.*)
5. status (*n.*)

   a. to understand something
   b. condition at a particular time
   c. connected with money or how money is managed
   d. the continuous movement of something from one place to another
   e. money you need to buy something

Task 4 Ask each other

e.g.   A: What does 'cost' mean?
       B: It means ...

Task 5 Send a message on social media using the above words

e.g.   We should have a grasp of stock market trends.

2. Preview — Accounting & financial reports

 Task 6 **Listen and read**

077

Accounting is the process of recording all of a company's financial activities. Using these accounting records, the company prepares financial reports to check information related to its financial condition, including the sales amounts, materials costs, profits, debts, and assets. The major financial statements are profit and loss (P&L) statements, balance sheets, and cash flow statements. P&L statements reveal the company's profit during a certain fiscal year. Balance sheets show the company's financial status including all the assets or debts at the end of the fiscal year. Cash flow statements record how much cash has flowed into and out of the company during a given period. Having enough cash increases the credibility of the company. These three financial statements are used to check a company's financial status.

Q3 Why do companies need P&L statements, balance sheets, and cash flow statements?

 Task 7 **Listen and fill in the blanks**

078

Each company decides its ($^{1.}$) year, and it settles its financial records at the end of this period. Based on the ($^{2.}$) rules, each company has to prepare some financial statements such as a ($^{3.}$) and loss (P&L) statement and a ($^{4.}$) sheet for the fiscal year. A company is responsible for reporting its financial ($^{5.}$) to the banks that they borrowed ($^{6.}$) from, and the shareholders investing in it. Financial statements are important for the company to make plans and decide the investment ($^{7.}$) for the next year. The information in these documents must be accurate as they are ($^{8.}$) related to the company's future plans.

Task 8 **Share your thoughts in pairs**

Q4 Which stakeholders need to see a company's P&L statements, balance sheets, and cash flow statements, and why?

e.g. I think the investors need them because they need to check the company's performance.

Q5 You are the owner of a café. What are the costs of running this café?

e.g. I think electricity is one of the costs for a café owner. Another cost is purchasing coffee beans.

3. Topics — The importance of financial management

Task 9 Read and discuss each question with your classmates

079

Good financial management is critical for business success. Quite a few start-ups cease their business in the first few years due to a lack of cash. When you run your own business, having a grasp of financial figures will help you avoid failure in business management. That is, you should learn a lot more about the three important financial statements: profit and loss (P&L) statements, balance sheets, and cash flow statements. In this reading, let's learn mainly about P&L statements, which show how much sales the company generated, how much it spent on costs and expenses, then how much profit or loss it made during a specific time period.

Q6 What do you learn from the P&L statement?

080

Below you can see the kinds of income and expense information a company or firm lists on the P&L statement. The P&L statement shows the total profit and loss of the company or firm in a specific period. It is usually published monthly, quarterly, semi-annualy, and annually for management, investors, creditors, and other stakeholders outside of the company. The P&L statement details the money flowing in and out and helps you understand what is behind a company's profitability by categorizing profits and expenses.

The P&L statement

Net sales	純売上高①	ある一定期間の売上高（返品や値引き分等は含まない純粋な製品・サービスの売上）
Cost of goods sold (COGS)	売上原価②	売れた品の原材料コスト
Gross profit (loss)	**売上総利益（損失）③**	**売上高—売上原価＝売上総利益（粗利）[①−②＝③]**
Selling, general & administrative expenses (SG & A)	販売費及び一般管理費④	販売にかかる費用や、それ以外の一般的な管理にかかる費用
Operating profit (loss)	**営業利益（損失）⑤**	**本業で稼いだ利益　[③−④＝⑤]**
Non-operating income	営業外利益⑥	企業が本業以外（賃料等）で稼いだ利益
Non-operating expenses	営業外費用⑦	本業以外でかかった費用（利息支払い等）
Ordinary profit (loss)	**経常利益（損失）⑧**	**経常的な活動で得た利益　[⑤＋⑥−⑦＝⑧]**
Extraordinary income	特別利益⑨	企業の臨時的な利益（不動産売却益など）
Extraordinary loss	特別損失⑩	企業の臨時・突発的な損失（災害損失等）
Profit (loss) before tax	**税引前利益（損失）⑪**	**税金を支払う前の利益　[⑧＋⑨−⑩＝⑪]**
Income taxes	法人税等⑫	法人税等
Net profit (loss)	**当期純利益（損失）⑬**	**税金等も引いた後の最終的な利益[⑪−⑫＝⑬]**

Q7 What is the structure of a P&L statement?

081 The word 'sales' means income from selling the products or services a company provides. 'Costs of Goods Sold (COGS)' are the direct costs of producing and selling goods or services, such as materials, labor, shipping, and freight costs. 'Expenses' are the money spent to generate income. There are different types of operating expenses that a company generates, including salaries and wages, rent, utilities, insurance, marketing, and advertising. There are 5 different levels of profits in the P&L. For instance, gross profit can be calculated by the formula 'sales − COGS.'

Q8 Compare the performances of the following two companies using the P&L statements. What differences do you notice?

082 The following are P&L statements of two companies, A and B, in the same industry.

The P&L statement for Company A and Company B

Company A (P&L)

Net sales	5,500
Cost of goods sold (COGS)	800
Gross profit	4,700
Selling, general, and administrative expenses (SG&A)	4,150
Operating profit	550
Ordinary profit	300
Net profit	280

Company B (P&L)

Net sales	7,700
Cost of goods sold (COGS)	1,200
Gross profit	6,500
Selling, general, and administrative expenses (SG&A)	5,800
Operating profit	700
Ordinary profit	400
Net profit	380

We can check a company's performance by looking at the amount of sales and profit on a P&L statement. However, in most cases, when a company is larger, the amounts of sales and profit are also larger. If people compare two companies with just the actual numbers of sales and profit, they may think the company which earns larger sales is performing better. To avoid this misunderstanding, a profit margin ratio is often used to compare companies' performances in the same industry. A profit margin ratio is the amount of profit as a percentage of net sales. It can measure the degree of effectiveness with which a company's activities make money by dividing the profits by the sales, as profits are the leftover of sales after deducting the costs and expenses of the company. If a company spends too much on costs or expenses, the ratio will go down. Calculating the profit margin ratio allows people to compare companies of different sizes and situations. You can calculate the profit margin using the formula:

profit ÷ sales × 100 = profit margin ratio (%)

Q9 Do you understand why financial statements are important for a company? How are those financial statements shared with the company's stakeholders?

🎧 083 There are two other financial statements: balance sheets and cash flow statements. The balance sheets display a company's total assets and how these assets are financed. They can also be referred to as 'the statements of net worth' or 'the statements of financial position.' The balance sheet is based on the following equation: assets = liabilities + equity. The cash flow statements tell you how much cash flowed in and out of a company during a given period. They show the source of cash and help you monitor the flow of money. There are three sections in cash flow statements: operating activities, investments, and financial activities.

Task 10 **What interests you most in this article? Write down your ideas.**

コラム❶　　　**会社のお金あれこれ** ―損益計算書（P&L）と貸借対照表（BS）

　「決算」とは、一会計期間における企業の経営成績と期末の財務状況を確認することで、作成される書類一式を「決算書」と言います。「損益計算書」、「貸借対照表」も決算書に含まれます。「損益計算書（Profit & Loss statement, P&L）」は、収益から費用を差し引き、その残りを利益（儲け）として表します。「貸借対照表（Balance Sheet, BS）」は、期末における企業の財政状態を示し、左側に「資産の部」（資金の運用状況）、右側にその資金の調達元（「負債の部」：借入、「純資産の部」：自己資本）を示します。貸借対照表は、「資産＝負債＋純資産」となるため、バランスシートとも呼ばれます。経営者は、これらの財務諸表を分析し、経営改善を行います。

4. Useful words and phrases for business

Task 11 Listen and do shadowing

084

words & phrases	sample sentences
accounting 会計、簿記	He is the manager of the **accounting** department.
assets 資産	The company has 30 billion dollars in **assets**.
profit and loss statement 損益計算書	You need to understand the **profit and loss statement** if you want to run your business.
cash flow statement キャッシュフロー計算書	The **cash flow statement** is an important financial statement in business.
balance sheet 貸借対照表	A **balance sheet** provides a snapshot of assets and liabilities at a certain time.
credibility 信頼性	That company needs to regain its **credibility** in the market.
cease 止む、終わる	The company **ceased** the operation of all trains due to heavy snow.
failure 失敗、不成功	That agreement was a complete **failure** for our business.
insight 洞察力	You need deep **insights** to become an entrepreneur.
obligation 義務	If you sign a contract, you have an **obligation** to carry out this project.
liability 責任、負債	The president denied **liability** for the damage his company caused.
convert 変える、転換する	People are encouraged to **convert** their goods into cash at this flea market.
creditor 債権者、貸し主	As that company went bankrupt, many **creditors** rushed into the business.
stakeholder 出資者	Corporate executives have to create value for customers and **stakeholders**.

 Task 12 For more details, check an online English-English dictionary

1. Use a smartphone or the Internet
2. Select an online English-English dictionary
3. Look up the word(s)
4. Check the results and share ideas with your classmates

5. Research project and discussion

Task 13 **Do research on P&L statements in groups**

The following tables show the P&L statements of the two companies. When comparing them, what do you see? What are the big differences in the profits and costs between these two companies? Calculate their profit margins and check how the two companies are handling their finances.

The P&L of X machinery Co., Ltd. (¥ million)

Net sales	9,800
Cost of goods sold (COGS)	6,500
Gross profit	3,300
Selling, General, and Administrative expenses (SG&A)	2,500
Operating profit	800
Ordinary profit	700
Net profit	600

The P&L of Z networks Co., Ltd. (¥ million)

Net sales	9,500
Cost of goods sold (COGS)	1,000
Gross profit	8,500
Selling, General, and Administrative expenses (SG&A)	3,000
Operating profit	5,500
Ordinary profit	4,000
Net profit	3,500

Next, find the P&L statements for a company on the Internet in the last two years, and see whether their businesses have improved or declined using what you have learned about financial statements.

Task 14 **Make a presentation about the P&L statements you found**

Which presentation is most impressive?

コラム ❷

損益計算書から経営改善ポイントを見つけよう！
～企業の本業で稼ぐ力～

　利益で売上高を割った「売上高利益率」は、売上高に対する利益の割合（margin）で、企業のパフォーマンスを測る指標です。中でも、売上高（sales）から原価（cost of goods sold: COGS）と販売管理費（販管費：selling, general, and administrative expense: SG & A）を引いた営業利益（operating profit）を使う営業利益率（operating profit margin）は、企業の「本来ビジネス」における収益力の指標です。モノやヒトをあまり必要としないビジネスであれば、原価と販費は低いため、営業利益率は高くなります。例えば、ネット銀行は店舗や人員が不要なため、リアル店舗の銀行より営業利益率は高くなると考えられます。また、必ず原材料が必要な製造業では、原材料の費用削減ができれば、営業利益率は上がるでしょう。このように、利益率は、ビジネスにおける改善点を見出す指標になるのです。

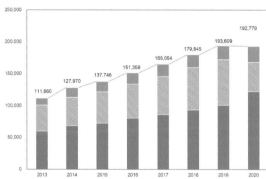

Changes in the scale of the Business-to-Consumer [B to C] EC market over the years

(unit: 100 million yen)

▮ Scale of the B-to-C EC market in the merchandising sector

▮ Scale of the B-to-C EC market in the service sector

▮ Scale of the B-to-C EC market in the digital sector

Source: Website of the Ministry of Economy, Trade and Industry of Japan (https://www.meti.go.jp/english/press/2021/0730_002.html)

Warmup

Task 1 **Share ideas in English and Japanese**

E-commerce has become a common practice for businesses. The expansion of the Internet from young to elderly people, and the development of portable digital devices have made e-commerce familiar to everybody.

Q1 Do you know anything about e-commerce? What is e-commerce?

e.g. E-commerce is online shopping, like Amazon.

Q2 Look at the graph above. It shows survey results about e-commerce in Japan. What kind of information do you see?

経営の４つの資源でもある「情報」は、私たちの生活に必要不可欠なものとなりました。例えば、電子商取引（Electric Commerce, e-commerce, EC）があります。日常で利用する機会の多いネットショッピングは、電子商取引（Ｅコマース）の１つです。Ｅコマースは、インターネット上に市場を創り出しました。また、Ｅコマースと従来の商業活動の融合も大きなビジネス・チャンスとなっています。ネット販売では、商品を配送するための物流が不可欠です。また、実店舗においても無人レジ、電子決済等が普及しつつあります。そこに様々な情報のマネジメントが存在しています。

1. Familiarize yourself with business words and phrases

Computer hardware encompasses digital devices such as desktop computers, laptop computers, mobile phones, and tablet computers. Digital tools are programs, websites, or online resources. They can be accessed in web browsers at home as well as at work.

Task 2 **Brainstorm with your classmates**

What kind of devices do you use to browse the Internet? Why do you choose these devices? What kinds of social media or other apps do you use to communicate?

e.g. I use a tablet most because the size of a tablet is suitable for me to study. I often use chat apps.

Task 3 **Match each word with the definition**

1. e-commerce (*n.*)
2. domestic (*adj.*)
3. transaction (*n.*)
4. consumer (*n.*)
5. recently (*adv.*)
6. rapidly (*adv.*)

a. a business action such as buying or selling
b. lately or nowadays
c. very quickly
d. inside one country
e. a person who purchases or uses goods or services
f. buying and selling goods on the Internet

Task 4 **Ask each other**

e.g. A: What does 'e-commerce' mean?
B: It means ...

Task 5 **Send a message on social media using the above words**

e.g. Consumers are always in pursuit of products that are reasonably priced, high quality, or both.

2. Preview — Digitalization of people's lives in Japan

Task 6 Listen and read

085

As digitalization is rapidly expanding, digital devices and tools have become an indispensable part of our lives. According to a survey on telecommunications usage during the COVID-19 pandemic in 2020, more than 95% of households own mobile devices. Look at the graph on the right. It shows the use of digital devices. 89.4% of the respondents use smartphones, 26.5% of them use tablets, 48.5% of them use laptop computers, and 20.9% of them use desktop computers. Digital devices and tools are used in all aspects of our personal lives and all types of workplaces.

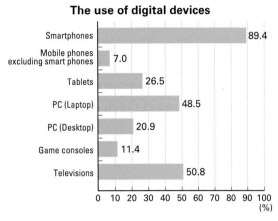

The use of digital devices

出典：総務省 (2021)「ウィズコロナにおけるデジタル活用の実態と利用者意識の変化に関する調査研究」

Q3   Think about what else you can read from this graph. What digital devices and tools are you using? Why? If you don't use them, why not?

Task 7 Listen and fill in the blanks

086

Amazon opened Amazon Go stores in the US in (1.   ). The stores had no (2.   ) registers. Customers enter the store, open the app, tap 'In-Store Code,' and check in with the QR code (3.   ). Then customers can shop by themselves. They just browse and pick the goods (4.   ) they would at any other store. They have no more cashiers, no registers, and no (5.   ) lines. Throughout the store, a combination of numerous cameras, weight sensors, and voice microphones are (6.   ) on the shelves, walls, and ceilings in order to capture customers' movements. Then, the store sends a bill to the credit card registered in the app. New (7.   ) technologies have made it possible for Amazon to open these (8.   ) stores. This system has the potential to completely change the (9.   ) industry. It might mean big changes are coming for supermarket businesses.

総務省 (2020)「O2O から OMO へ」．『令和 2 年度情報通信白書』．pp.284-285. を加筆修正の上、作成。

Task 8 Share your thoughts in pairs

Q4   What do you think about Amazon Go stores? Do you want to use them?

e.g.   I am interested in using such a store because we can save time with the checkout.

Q5   Do you have any concerns about digital shopping? Are you using any payment apps?

e.g.   I have concerns about digital shopping. I sometimes hear about some troubles.

3. Topics — What can companies do with ICT?

> **Task 9** **Read and discuss each question with your classmates**

087 The decreasing working-age population due to aging, a declining general population, and a decreased birthrate will likely cause ever-smaller labor input. In addition, falling productivity gains on a per-worker basis could bring about a worse economy and labor situation in the future.

Q6 Quality of life (QoL) often includes vitality, health, well-being, happiness, leisure, and income. Do you think ICT can improve your QoL?

088

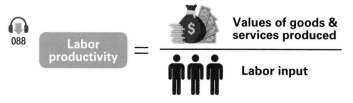

$$\text{Labor productivity} = \frac{\text{Values of goods \& services produced}}{\text{Labor input}}$$

Based on The Ministry of General Affairs

If the adoption of ICT is able to increase labor productivity per worker, ICT should help ease labor shortage problems due to the declining population. Moreover, ICT is hoped to improve the population's QoL, and then stop the flow of people from outlying regions to urban centers. In addition, ICT should help maintain and enhance regional dynamism. Organizing the expectations for ICT's role in solving social issues allows us to redefine and summarize those expectations into the following points.

Q7 In terms of the following points, what can ICT help with?

089 **Labor quality** — The automation of routine operations by adopting Robotic Process Automation (RPA) and other types of ICT should make companies' operations more efficient. What is more, ICT enables companies to set up working conditions that let workers focus on more productive work.

Regional population — Japan's local regions are dealing with a lack of leaders and supporters due to falling and aging populations and declining birthrates. Each region needs to involve people from outside the region as its ardent fans, who help with community building. In other words, the number of people engaged with the region increases. ICT applications will support regional areas in disseminating information and forming relationships that will lead to engagement with more people.

Work opportunities — Teleworking, crowdsourcing, avatar robots, and other forms of ICT allow people to work from nearly any location. In this way, ICT gives more work opportunities to people who otherwise find it hard to work due to other factors, such as childcare, caregiving, or disability.

Markets — ICT can enable businesses to supply products and services matching the various needs of consumers in regions all over the world, even in small local markets. ICT is also expected to increase market sizes by expanding business possibilities beyond the supply of goods. For example, if businesses can use 5G, they can more easily connect to remote locations and provide many online services. Also, ICT will make it easier for customers to pay when shopping online as well as visiting real shops.

Q8 Digitalization is essential today. What is a digital transformation (DX)?

090

ICT can help companies effectively improve the digitalization of their business processes. Digitalization refers to the changing of all business processes from analog to digital form. Furthermore, companies have their eyes on the concept of digital transformation (DX). DX means that companies adapt to dramatic internal and external environmental changes

by creating new products and services, offering customers totally new experiences by utilizing digital technologies. DX may provide distractive changes not only to companies but also to the entire society. On the other hand, it may cause drastic changes in the power balance among companies in markets. This is also called digital disruption. However, if companies meet the needs of DX, it may be a strong competitive advantage for them in the near future.

Q9 How well is cashless payment accepted in Japan? Do you think it will become more popular?

091

Mobile payments have become much more popular in recent years. More and more people have come to use smartphone apps, which have made remarkable progress. However, although cashless payments made up 40 to 60% of purchases in major countries in 2017, the proportion in Japan was only about 30% in 2020. The Japanese government is trying to improve the convenience and efficiency of payments through the expansion of cashless payments, aiming to change 40% of all payments in Japan to cashless payments by the end of June 2025. However, there are still some debates about the benefits of a cashless society.

Cashless payment in Japan (2019)

	Pre-Paid	Real-time payment		Post-payment
Example of services	electric money (rechargeable passes or cards issued by companies)	debit card	mobile wallet (using QR codes)	credit card
Features	charge money in advance	withdraw in real time	withdraw in real time	pay later
Payment method	non-contact touching	with card reader	* with camera (reading QR or bar codes) * non-contact touching	with card reader
% of payments in private consumption expenditure in Japan (2019)	1.9%	0.56%	0.31%	24.0%

出典：経済産業省「キャッシュレス・ビジョン」令和2年版情報通信白書第1部を加筆修正の上、翻訳

Q10 Why have cashless payments had difficulties gaining wide acceptance?

092

There are several reasons why cashless payments are still not popular in Japan: (1) few thefts and a safe society, (2) cash being trusted widely, (3) quick and accurate cash register processing at stores, and (4) the convenience of ATMs. Another reason is the high switching costs required for stores and other merchants to introduce cashless payment, such as the costs of installing terminals, training, and maintenance. In addition, cashless payments may cause cash flow problems because of the time lag between payments and the receipt of funds after settlement. On the other hand, the cost of maintaining the current cash settlement infrastructure is estimated to be more than 1 trillion yen per year in direct expenses, including printing, transportation, store installation, the cost of ATMs, and labor. There is a growing demand to reduce the costs associated with handling cash to improve the efficiency of our society. Furthermore, it would also help to offset the shortage of labor in stores due to the declining population.

* 本章 Topics (pp.84-86) の英文は、2019年（令和元年）～ 2021年（令和三年）の総務省『情報通信白書』およびその英語版の一部を加筆修正の上、作成。詳細は、巻末参考文献一覧を参照。

Task 10 **What interests you most in this article? Write down your ideas.**

コラム❶

リープフロッグ現象と日本のデジタル化を阻むもの

　令和2年版情報通信白書（総務省）では、「日本は利便性が高いからこそ、デジタル化が進まない」という可能性が指摘されています。例として、タクシーがすぐ捕まるのでライドシェアが進まない、現金の信頼性が高い点からキャッシュレスが浸透しないなどです。逆にアフリカ諸国などではスマートフォン普及率が100％を超える国もあり、これまでインフラ整備が遅れていたからこそ、急速に日常生活やビジネスでのデジタル化が一気に進みつつあると言われます。これは「リープフロッグ現象（Leapfrog）」と呼ばれ、これまでのように段階的な発展を経ずに、いきなり ICT を活用し、ダイナミックに発展することを指します。

4. Useful words and phrases for business

 Task 11 **Listen and do shadowing**

093

words & phrases	sample sentences
indispensable 絶対必要な	He is an **indispensable** member of the project team.
terminals 端末	The **terminals** of the online system were down yesterday.
numerous 多数の	We had **numerous** applicants this year.
capture 獲得する	His work **captured** the boss's attention.
decline 減退する	The price of this item has **declined** since last year.
be bound to 〜する義務がある	Employees **are bound to** report their mistakes immediately.
reduction 縮小、下落	Our positive campaign was able to contribute to cost **reduction**.
stem (v.) (流れを)せき止める	They must take action to **stem** the tide of resignations.
outlying 中心を離れた、遠い	In **outlying** areas, many outlet shopping malls have opened.
dynamism 力強さ	The **dynamism** of Japanese Kabuki attracted the European audience.
redefine 再定義する	This PC software can **redefine** tables and charts instantly.
ardent 熱烈な、熱心な	There are many **ardent** fans of this product in the U.S.
disseminate ばらまく、広める	The CEO **disseminated** information in order to raise our company's reputation.
diffuse 普及する	The good smell was **diffused** throughout the room.
offset 相殺する	Domestic losses were **offset** by developing foreign markets.

 Task 12 **For more details, check an online English-English dictionary**

1. Use a smartphone or the Internet
2. Select an online English-English dictionary
3. Look up the word(s)
4. Check the results and share ideas with your classmates

5. Research project and discussion

Task 13 **Do research on words related to business and technology in groups**

Choose one of the following topics and do research on the Internet.

Artificial Intelligence (AI) — intelligent machines which work like human brains

Blockchain — a database that is shared among the nodes of a computer network

Data protection and security — the process of protecting important information

Digital automation – applying new technologies to businesses

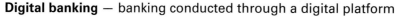

Digital banking — banking conducted through a digital platform

5G — the 5th generation mobile network

Hybrid workplace — a flexible working model allowing employees to work in the workplace or a remote location

Task 14 **Make a presentation about a digital transformation**

Which presentation is most impressive?

コラム ❷

デジタルトランスフォーメーション（DX）とは

　昨今、デジタルトランスフォーメーション（DX）という言葉をよく聞くようになりました。従来は ICT（Information and Communication Technology）という言葉が一般的でしたが、ICT はあくまで効率化やビジネスの価値向上のためのツールでした。一方、DX とは産業そのものに ICT が組み込まれ、ビジネスのあり方自体が変わることを意味します。

従来の情報化／ICT利活用　　　　デジタルトランスフォーメーション

データが価値の源泉に
経済活動のコスト構造が変革

ICTは、確立された産業の
効率化や価値の向上を
実現化する補助ツール

ICT は、産業と一体化することで、
ビジネスモデル自体を変革する
事業のコアとなる

総務省（2020）.『令和元年版情報通信白書』を参照し作成。
https://www.soumu.go.jp/johotsusintokei/whitepaper/ja/r01/html/nb000000.html

Chapter 12

Including the SDGs in business

SDGsとビジネス

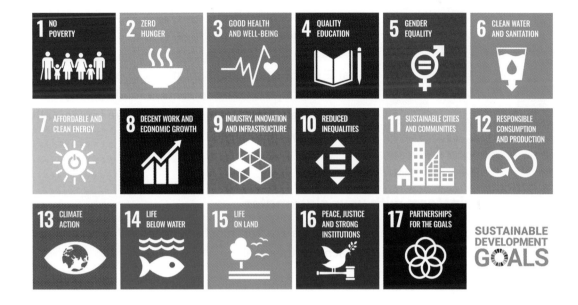

Warmup

Task 1 **Share ideas in English and Japanese**

ESG (Environment, Social, and Governance) investments prioritizing sustainability have shown rapid growth. Since the UN adopted the SDGs (Sustainable Development Goals), today, companies around the world are focusing their efforts on incorporating them into their management.

Q1 What kinds of products or services around you seem to be related to the SDGs?

Q2 What kind of strengths can companies display in the midst of this trend sweeping the world?

常に最新のテクノロジーで、新しい市場が創出されています。一方、社会が豊かになる中で、これまで様々な地球上の環境、そして人々（労働力）も浪費されてきました。今、その改善と並行し、ビジネスでも持続可能性を重視するESG投資に急速な拡大が見られます。2015年には国連サミットで、グローバルな社会課題を解決し持続可能な世界を実現するための目標であるSDGs（持続可能な開発目標：Sustainable Development Goals）が採択されました。現在、世界の企業はSDGsを取り入れた経営に注力しつつあります。また日本企業でも、SDGsはビジネスの目標と関連して掲げられ、SDGsを取り入れたビジネスの可能性はますます広がっています。

1. Familiarize yourself with business words and phrases

Goal 2: End hunger, achieve food security and improved nutrition, and promote sustainable agriculture.

Goal 2 seeks sustainable solutions to end hunger in all its forms by 2030 and to achieve food security. The aim is to ensure that everyone everywhere has enough good-quality food to lead healthy lives.

Task 2 Brainstorm with your classmates

Which specific goal(s) among the 17 SDGs are you most interested in? What actions in your daily life are you taking to achieve this goal?

e.g. I know only two of them, no poverty and quality education. I am interested in climate action. I think I can use the air conditioning less to avoid CO_2 emissions.

Task 3 Match each word with the definition

1. advocate (*n.*)
2. sustainability (*n.*)
3. hunger (*n.*)
4. incorporate (*v.*)
5. sweep (*v.*)
6. midst (*n.*)

a. to move quickly
b. to include something as part of a whole
c. the middle of something
d. a person who publicly supports something
e. an uneasy feeling due to lacking foods to eat
f. the ability to continue over a while

Task 4 Ask each other

e.g. A: What does 'sustainability' mean?
B: It means ...

Task 5 Send a message on social media using the above words

e.g. I heard a European fashion trend is sweeping Asia.

2. Preview — SDGs as a business activity

 Task 6 **Listen and read**

094

To achieve the SDGs all over the world, investment is necessary in the range of 5 to 7 trillion dollars per year. This means that we need a large amount of investment money that remains unfulfilled. For corporations, industries, or companies, investing in the SDGs might involve unavoidable risks, but it can also present great opportunities to create and capture markets in the future. Now, many people around the world are working to achieve the SDGs. Working to achieve the SDGs through business strengthens a corporation's foundation for sustainability and offers opportunities to win massive untapped markets. If they are afraid of risks and don't work on the SDGs, they might harm their reputation and customers might choose not to buy their products anymore. However, if they take risks and try to help achieve the SDGs, their business models could lead to the growth of these markets.

Q3 Do you know any Japanese companies which support the SDGs? What are they doing to achieve the SDGs?

 Task 7 **Listen and fill in the blanks**

095

Sumitomo Chemical, a Japanese company, has contributed to the SDGs in (¹.   ). The company developed a (².   ) for the social good. It is a mosquito net (*Kaya*) named *Olyset® Net* which keeps pests such as mosquitos out of (³.   ). The net blocks and kills these bad insects using insecticides, or insect-killing substances. Thanks to such mosquito (⁴.   ), many people have stopped feeling afraid of getting malaria. This net is supplied to over (⁵.   ) countries via UNICEF and other international organizations. In (⁶.   ), the company has created local employment and contributed to the development of the local (⁷.   ). This work has created nearly (⁸.   ) employment opportunities in Tanzania.

写真提供：住友化学株式会社

経済産業省 (2019). "Practice 9. Innovation with Olyset® Nets (Sumitomo Chemical Company, Limited)." *The Guide for SDG Business Management.* を加筆修正の上、作成。

Task 8 **Share your thoughts in pairs**

Q4 In Africa, do you know about other Japanese companies' activities or businesses?

e.g. I've heard that a company named Saraya Co.,Ltd. contributes to Africa by selling sanitizer.

Q5 Have you ever participated in SDG-related activities? If you have, what did you do? Please share your experience with your classmates.

3. Topics — SDGs and business

Task 9 Read and discuss each question with your classmates

096
Recently investors want to know more about a company's future value, rather than simply focusing on past performance. The question many investors ask is, "Does the vision presented by a company match the future vision for society?" ESG criteria and the SDGs are the standards or indicators we can use to answer this question.

Q6 Why do investors want to know about each company's future vision for the SDGs?

097
Investors are interested in the company's ideas about how they would like to contribute to the sustainability of the world. Investors think the ideas are also important for a company to make its business sustainable in the future. Recently, the term ESG is often used in communication between companies and investors. Companies often say, "We are engaged in long-term activities." However, this isn't clear enough. For investors, the long-term vision of a company is most important, so what it is trying to aim for in the future should be presented in detail. Investors value this kind of information. ESG management has become one of the most important factors for investors when evaluating a company.

Q7 Why do companies think about their employees and customers when considering ESG business management and the SDGs?

098
When considering ESG business management, companies can't ignore employees and customers. An increasing number of people are familiar with the SDGs, and they are paying more attention to whether companies are trying to contribute. By supporting the SDGs, companies can promote more employee engagement and attract more customers. It is very important that employees recognize how their jobs connect to all 17 SDGs. To help with this, management issues related to the SDGs could be included in integrated reports and made open to the companies' stakeholders. If employees become aware of their roles in helping achieve the SDGs, then the SDGs might be endorsed by even more companies. Indeed, taking action to achieve the SDGs could motivate many young people. As you can see, there are many benefits for companies that clearly and specifically show their vision regarding the SDGs.

Q8 What are the keys for companies to achieve the SDGs?

099
In order to achieve each of the 17 SDGs, it is necessary for companies to strengthen their core competence by including various resources and stakeholders' perspectives in the management process. If a company and stakeholders are in harmony, they can form a powerful driving force to solve many global problems. It is also very important that companies collaborate with the government and other industries. Collaboration is key and the SDGs make it easier for larger companies to collaborate with start-ups and innovate something new together because they can start from the same baseline understanding. Society is changing in such a way that major corporations can gain knowledge and resources from start-up companies.

Q9 What kind of activities do companies do to help achieve the SDGs?

100
Many companies are now trying to take the idea of ESG into consideration in their business while meeting the SDGs. For example, they are trying to reduce the waste causing environmental pollution. In June 2019, the leaders of the G20 Osaka Summit shared the Osaka Blue Ocean Vision, which is a project that targets the reduction of additional pollution by marine plastic litter to zero by 2050. To achieve this target, the engagement of many countries around the world will be necessary. Of course, many Japanese companies are also trying to reduce the amount of plastic litter in the ocean.

Another example is the case of the PILOT Corporation, a famous pen manufacturer. This corporation made a commitment to stakeholders to address marine plastic waste and launched the "Super Grip G Ocean Plastic" oil-based ballpoint pen. It uses reclaimed resin from marine plastic waste collected in Japan, in collaboration with TerraCycle Japan. By using recycled materials from marine plastic waste for their products, PILOT Corporation is showing their stakeholders that their vision aligns with the SDGs.

Super Grip G Ocean Plastic

写真提供：PILOT Corporation

Q10 What kind of new values do the SDGs give businesses?

Focusing on the SDGs can be an opportunity to address markets that have been ignored by companies from the perspective of economic rationality. The true embodiment of SDG business management is to boldly pioneer new markets and balance problem-solving with business by collaborating with other companies and academia, mobilizing new technology and knowledge. It is essential that top executives maintain that long-term perspective as they make their commitments and deliver their messages. When considering roles for companies in the SDGs and ideas of ESG, it is a prerequisite that the company itself be sustainable.

* 本章 Topics (pp.92-94) の英文は、経済産業省 (2019). *The Guide for SDG Business Management.* および環境省 (2021). *Annual Report on the Environment in Japan 2021.* の一部を加筆修正の上、作成。詳細は、巻末参考文献一覧を参照。

Task 10 **What interests you most in this article? Write down your ideas.**

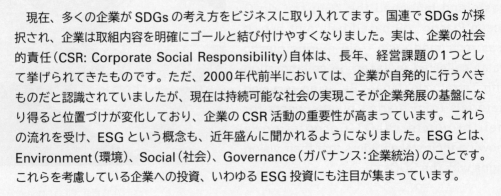

コラム❶

企業の社会的責任（CSR）と SDGs

　現在、多くの企業が SDGs の考え方をビジネスに取り入れてます。国連で SDGs が採択され、企業は取組内容を明確にゴールと結び付けやすくなりました。実は、企業の社会的責任（CSR: Corporate Social Responsibility）自体は、長年、経営課題の1つとして挙げられてきたものです。ただ、2000 年代前半においては、企業が自発的に行うべきものだと認識されていましたが、現在は持続可能な社会の実現こそが企業発展の基盤になり得ると位置づけが変化しており、企業の CSR 活動の重要性が高まっています。これらの流れを受け、ESG という概念も、近年盛んに聞かれるようになりました。ESG とは、Environment（環境）、Social（社会）、Governance（ガバナンス：企業統治）のことです。これらを考慮している企業への投資、いわゆる ESG 投資にも注目が集まっています。

4. Useful words and phrases for business

Task 11 Listen and do shadowing

102

words & phrases	sample sentences
ESG 環境の、社会的、ガバナンスの	The **ESG** concept is a way of evaluating a company.
immensity 莫大、無数	The **immensity** of the role of a manager is unbelievable.
inevitably 必然的に	**Inevitably**, that leader will reconstruct the organization.
common language 共通言語	People working at this company use English as a **common language**.
permeate 浸透する	Dissatisfaction with the CEO seems to have **permeated** every section of the company.
take action 行動を起こす、取り掛かる	We are required to **take action** immediately when something goes wrong.
millennials ミレニアル世代	There are many **millennials** in our company.
multi-stakeholders マルチステークホルダー	Our manager attended the conference as a member of the **multi-stakeholder** committee.
utmost 最大の	We should take the **utmost** care of every client.
tremendous とてつもない	These solutions provide **tremendous** benefits from the very beginning.
with regard to に関して	**With regard to** this proposal, we will investigate it in more detail.
rationality 合理性	We are likely to interpret economic **rationality** in connection with profits.
embodiment 実施形態、体現	The president is the **embodiment** of power, creation, and generosity.
boldly 大胆に	The manager **boldly** cut the expenses for this fiscal year by 30%.
mobilize 動員する、結集する	The United Nations stressed the need to **mobilize** funding for the refugees.

 ### Task 12 For more details, check an online English-English dictionary

1. Use a smartphone or the Internet
2. Select an online English-English dictionary
3. Look up the word(s)
4. Check the results and share ideas with your classmates

5. Research project and discussion

Task 13 **Do research on the SDGs and business in groups**

The SDG Business Forum took place at the United Nations in 2017. At the Forum, private sector institutions and networks published a business statement on the opportunity and importance of the SDGs. The following is part of the business statement:

> "The SDGs provide all businesses with a new lens through which to translate the world's needs and ambitions into business solutions. These solutions will enable companies to better manage their risks, anticipate consumer demand, build positions in growth markets, secure access to needed resources, and strengthen their supply chains, while moving the world towards a sustainable and inclusive development path."

https://iccwbo.org/media-wall/news-speeches/business-stepping-transformational-partnerships/

Try to make a business plan which addresses the SDGs.

Task 14 **Make a presentation about the SDGs and business**

Which presentation is most impressive?

コラム ❷

グリーン調達とは

　グリーン調達とは、原材料や部品等を調達するときに、価格だけを考慮するのではなく、環境負荷の少ない原材料や、その配慮を行っているサプライヤーを選択することです。例えば、「環境にやさしい製品を製造しています」と明言するＡ社が、環境負荷を原材料調達では考慮していない場合、Ａ社の製品は真に環境にやさしいとは言えないでしょう。製造から廃棄まで、トータルで環境負荷の視点を取り入れて初めて、Ａ社は「環境にやさしい企業」「サスティナブルな企業」という価値を得ることができるのです、そのように考え、グリーン調達を意識する企業が増えています。

Task **Write a summary and share your feedback with each other.**
サマリーをまとめて、意見を共有しよう。

Tips for summarizing: Find a topic sentence in each paragraph and combine these topic sentences together, and you will write your summary.

Backstories:
Ethical fashion gains a foothold in Japan

Tamura Ginga

Puffer coats are a mainstay of winter. They're warm, cozy, and practical. And it's what's inside the lining that makes all the difference. Traditionally, down feathers from waterbirds have been used for insulation, but alternatives are growing more popular among consumers concerned about animal welfare and environmental sustainability.

Italian brand Save The Duck, has led the way. As its name suggests, the company does not use any waterbird feathers to make its signature jackets and vests.

Save The Duck was founded in the Italian fashion capital of Milan in 2012. CEO Nicolas Bargi has been a nature lover his whole life. He says he has always been skeptical about the use of actual waterbird feathers in jackets. After seeing many companies collapse as a result of the 2008 financial crisis and credit uncertainty in Europe, Bargi decided it was time for the fashion industry to change tack.

"I thought that there would have to be a big cultural and social change for people in the future, and sustainability would become a very strong factor for the new generation," he says.

©SAVE THE DUCK S.P.A

Bargi devised a way to recycle plastic bottles as an alternative to feathers. The bottles are broken down and mixed with polyester fibers. One jacket uses 20 bottles, instead of six to eight waterbirds.

And Save The Duck has quickly found there's an international demand for its products. It has expanded to 33 countries and territories, including Japan where it has launched a slew of pop-up stores nationwide.

Feather-free in Japan

In Japan, an entrepreneur from Osaka has turned to a tropical tree as another feather alternative. Fukai Kishow, the founder of KAPOK KNOT, started producing coats in 2019 that use material derived from kapok, a tree that grows in Southeast Asia, Central and South America, and Africa. The fluffy fibers taken from its seeds have historically

©KAPOK JAPAN

been used as stuffing for life jackets and soft toys. But it has not been widely used in clothing as its fibers are difficult to process.

Fukai, 29, visited Indonesia two years ago to choose fiber suitable for jackets. He worked with farmers and researchers to pick out the perfect material and signed sales contracts. He says Kapok fiber's excellent moisture absorption and thermal retention capacity make it warmer than other natural materials.

Kapok Knot coats come with a message in the packaging highlighting the low environmental impact of the production process. Fukai says he wants customers to appreciate the social value of his products.

"Enjoying fashion and thinking about the future are compatible," he says. "I want to pursue both business and social responsibility."

Vice-President of Japan Ethical Initiative, Ikoma Yoshiko, says ethical brands are set to become main players in the fashion industry.

"Investors have become increasingly critical of companies that do not consider environmental issues since the Sustainable Development Goals were adopted by the United Nations in 2015," she says. "I suppose fashion brands that are not environment-friendly will not be able to survive."

Ikoma has been tracking trends among younger consumers, particularly members of what is known as Generation Z. She says growing up with knowledge of climate change and other environmental issues has made them more sensitive of the effects of their spending decisions.

©KAPOK JAPAN

"I believe that similar to the 'digital transformation' in the business world, which makes use of the latest technology, the fashion industry will undergo an 'ethical transformation.'"

Source: NHK World-Japan, Monday, March 8, 2021
https://www3.nhk.or.jp/nhkworld/en/news/backstories/1533/

Task **Write a summary and share your feedback with each other.**

サマリーをまとめて、意見を共有しよう。

Tips for summarizing: Find a topic sentence in each paragraph and combine these topic sentences together, and you will write your summary.

Backstories:
Japanese artist finds value in E-waste

Ebara Miki

長坂真護氏

Tokyo-based artist Nagasaka Mago has been causing a real buzz of late. Despite the global pandemic, two exhibitions in Japan last year attracted more visitors than expected. He's inspired by the people who toil away in West Africa at one of the world's largest electronic dump sites. He uses the waste in his creations and spends the profits on the low-income community, such as providing gas masks for the workers and running a free school for children. He's living out his dreams and changing lives for the better, but isn't about to stop there.

Changed by Ghana

Sitting in a large studio in Tokyo's upscale Ginza district, Mago is able to laugh about his past struggles now. "Throughout my 20s, I was broke. All I wanted to do was paint, but my art wasn't selling. I was living with my single working mother, who would call me useless," he recalls.

It wasn't that he had zero talent back then. He was asked to paint live in public spaces and create installations for shopping centers, "but nothing was fulfilling", says the 36-year-old.

Looking for answers and inspiration, Mago decided to travel overseas, "making money from buying and selling digital devices."

One day, he was struck by a magazine photo of a little girl scavenging among a huge mountain of trash. "Growing up in Japan, I never knew people lived like that," he says.

Mago searched the internet for similar places, but it was Agbogbloshie in Ghana that resonated the most. "My inner voice told me I must visit." And so off he went on a journey that would forever transform his life and work.

The graveyard of E-waste

Agbogbloshie is not too far from the center of Ghana's capital, Accra. There's a big market that sells cheap food, but people from the city normally don't go beyond the market, into a huge slum — especially not tourists.

But Mago did. He says the jeers from the locals came thick and fast, and admits it was probably best he didn't understand what they meant. But one young man was kind enough to show him around the dump site.

"Its sheer size was incredible. Smoke was bellowing from the ground and a terrible smell filled the air," he remembers. Despite wearing a gas mask, it still gave him a headache.

Mago eventually befriended a group of guys known as the "burner boys," who get their name from the way they retrieve copper from cables and appliances. For 12 hours and just a few dollars per day, they risk their lives by inhaling copious amounts of hazardous smoke.

©MAGO CREATION

Looking down at all the waste, Mago remembered the things he once owned and then threw away without a care: laptops, video games, mobile phones and more. They could be in a mountain of waste just like this one, he thought — a place where children rummage all day, desperately looking for something to sell.

Mago stayed for nine days. Before he left, a burner boy asked if he'd ever come back — and to please bring some gas masks like his if he does, because "we don't want to die young".

Mago said he would. "But I was penniless. So I asked them if I could take some of the scrap they didn't need." He ended up carrying 50 kilograms of the stuff back to Japan. He then started to use the materials to create.

"The god of art smiled upon me"

Mago's first work since returning from Ghana depicted a burner boy turning into plastic. To the artist's amazement, it sold for more than 5,000 dollars. He was able to buy a return ticket to Agbogbloshie and convinced a company to donate 250 gas masks.

©MAGO CREATION

Five months later, he was back. He gave out the gas masks and picked up more scrap material for his works.

"It suddenly made sense to me — why I existed on this planet. It also became clear why my works never sold during my younger days. I didn't believe what art could do. I came to realize how art can help people. The god of art smiled upon me, and gave me this power," says Mago, who now receives regular shipments of unwanted scrap from Agbogbloshie.

©MAGO CREATION

The exhibitions he held in 2020 took place in two major department stores in Osaka and Nagoya. The dynamic works captivated those who visited, while many patrons said Mago's cause was a driving factor behind their decision to buy.

People who purchased Mago's artworks said they want to support his activities in Ghana.

Giving the kids a chance

These days, Mago pursues what he calls "sustainable capitalism." He explains the cycle, about how waste becomes valuable art. It can then be sold for a profit, which goes into the free school he set up in Ghana, or pays the wages of people who collect, process, and ship the scrap to him in Japan. What's more, the children create artworks of their own. These can be sold in Japan, and a portion of the proceeds will support their families.

『真実の湖 II』
©MAGO CREATION

"I must admit, I am a human of ambition and greed. We can't live like hermits. But even if we keep producing and consuming, it must be at least in a sustainable fashion," he says.

Mago describes the pandemic as a period of enlightenment, the chance to seek "that golden balance between the economy, the environment, and artistic creation."

Beyond art, he has his sights set on raising a major amount of funds to build an eco-friendly recycling factory in Agbogbloshie. That way, none of his friends will need to put their health at risk, and they'll be able to make enough money so that all the children can go to school. He hasn't been able to go back to Ghana in over a year due to the pandemic but has created hundreds of new paintings and sculptures.

"I promised all my friends in Ghana that I would come back again and again to achieve my goal. I'll keep my promise", he says with a smile.

Source: NHK World-Japan, Friday, Jan 22, 2021/
https://www3.nhk.or.jp/nhkworld/en/news/backstories/1471/

Glossary

Chapter 1

fulfill 満たす
tangible 実体的な
potential 見込みのある
revenue 総収入
play a key role 重要な役割を果たす
sanitation 衛生
visualize 視覚化する
consider 熟考する
define 定義する
lead 導く
identify 見極める
stack up 匹敵する
added value 付加価値
investor 投資家
critical 重要な
human resources 人的資源

Chapter 2

mission 使命
mission statement ミッションステートメント
mission-driven ミッションによる
social good 社会に良いこと
founder 創設者
aim 目的
define 定義する
get started 取りかかる
carry out 実行する
fall into 落ちる
focus on 注目する
stay on track 順調に物事を進める
adapt to 適応する
go through 詳細に見直す

Chapter 3

fundamental 基本の
external 外的の
sociological 社会学的な
legal 法律に関する
confirm 確認する
differentiation 差別化
profits 利益

modest 控えめな
strategic 戦略上の
systematic 系統的な
relevance 関連性
stability 安定
trade agreement 貿易協定
unemployment 失業
demographic 人口統計学の
innovative 革新的な

Chapter 4

aspect 面、見地
internal 内在的な
external 対外的な
consumer trends 消費者動向
counteract 逆らう、（反作用で）中和する
perspectives 考え方、見方
holistic 全体論の、全体の
assess 評価する、査定する
access アクセスする、利用する
obtain 得る
update 最新のものにする
perform 行う、実行する
prospect 予想、見通し

Chapter 5

distribute 分配する
e-commerce e コマース
decision-making 意思決定
fiscal year 会計年度
enterprise 企業
found 創設する
accumulate 積み重ねる
patent 特許
allocate 割り当てる
limit 制限する
expand 拡大する
handle 取り扱う
human resource management 人的資源管理

Chapter 6

demotivate やる気を失わせる
force 強いて～させる
delegate （権限などを）付与する
outcome(s) 結果、成果
straightforwardly あからさまに、率直に
enhance 高める
fulfill 果たす、満たす
social being 社会的存在
approve 賛成する、よいと認める
esteem needs 承認欲求
self-actualization 自己実現
hygiene factor 衛生要因
recognition 認識、認めること
empower 権限を与える
vital きわめて重要な

Chapter 7

supervisor 上司
applicant 応募者
emphasize 強調する
compensate 補う
indispensable 絶対必要な、避けられない
periodic 定期的な
era 時代

Chapter 8

fluctuating 変動する
skyrocket 急上昇する
segmentation 分割
presence 存在
distribution 流通
positioning （存在している）位置
manufacture 製造
potential 可能性
preference 好み
perception 認識
lightness 軽いこと
durability 耐久性
convey 伝える、伝達する

Chapter 9

health-conscious 健康志向の
intake 摂取
ordinary 普通の
flyer チラシ
high-end 最高仕様の
reasonable 適正の
available 利用可能な
suspicious 疑わしい
luxurious 豪華な、贅沢な
refrigeration 冷蔵

Chapter 10

accounting 会計、簿記
assets 資産
profit and loss statement 損益計算書
cash flow statement キャッシュフロー計算書
balance sheet 貸借対照表
credibility 信頼性
cease 止む、終わる
failure 失敗、不成功
insight 洞察力
obligation 義務
liability 責任、負債
convert 変える、転換する
creditor 債権者、貸し主
stakeholder 出資者

Chapter 11

indispensable 絶対必要な
terminals 端末
numerous 多数の
capture 獲得する
decline 減退する
be bound to ～する義務がある
reduction 縮小、下落
stem (v.) （流れを）せき止める
outlying 中心を離れた、遠い
dynamism 力強さ
redefine 再定義する
ardent 熱烈な、熱心な
disseminate ばらまく、広める

diffuse 普及する
offset 相殺する

Chapter 12

ESG 環境の、社会的、ガバナンスの
immensity 莫大、無数
inevitably 必然的に
common language 共通言語
permeate 浸透する
take action 行動を起こす、取り掛かる
philosophy 哲学
millennials ミレニアル世代
multi-stakeholders マルチステークホルダー
utmost 最大の
tremendous とてつもない
with regard to に関して
rationality 合理性
embodiment 実施形態、体現
boldly 大胆に
mobilize 動員する、結集する

References 参考文献

Chapter 1

Commonwealth of Australia (2020). *Guide to starting business.* Australian Government's Homepage (Business).
   https://business.gov.au/guide/starting/check-if-youre-ready
OpenStax (2018). *Introduction to Business.* Rice University.
   https://openstax.org/details/books/introduction-business
北居明・松本雄一・鈴木竜太・上野山達哉・島田善道 (2020).『経営学ファーストステップ』. 八千代出版.
榊原清則 (2013).『経営学入門（上）第 2 版』. 日本経済新聞出版.
（独）中小企業基盤整備機構 (n.d.).「ヒト・モノ・カネ・情報として計画を立てる～会社の 4 大経営資源を考える～」.『BCP
   はじめの一歩　事業継続力強化計画をつくろう！』.（独）中小企業基盤整備機構ホームページ.
   https://kyoujinnka.smrj.go.jp/guidance/04/

Chapter 2

Barney, J. B. (2002). *Gaining and Sustaining Competitive Advantage*, 2nd ed. Prentice-Hall.（岡田正大訳 (2003).『企業戦
   略論―競争優位の構築と持続上）』. ダイヤモンド社.）
Kotler, P. & Armstrong, G. (2012). *Principles of Marketing*, 14th ed. Prentice Hall.（コトラー，P.・アームストロング，G.・
   恩藏直人 (2014).『コトラー、アームストロング、恩藏のマーケティング原理』. 丸善出版.）
William, C. (May15, 2018). "The Importance of Having A Mission-Driven Company." *Forbes*.
   https://www.forbes.com/sites/williamcraig/2018/05/15/the-importance-of-having-a-mission-driven-
   company/?sh=264224693a9c
横川雅人 (2010).「現代日本企業の経営理念―「経営理念の上場企業実態調査」を踏まえて」.『産研論集』(37), 125-137.
（一社）関西経済同友会 企業経営委員会 (2020).「提言：経営者は「魅力ある企業」に向けた行動・仕組みづくりを～「人」
   を活かす経営による革新と成長を目指して～」. 関西経済同友会.
   https://www.kansaidoyukai.or.jp/wp-content/uploads/2020/04/200406_Maintext.pdf
労働政策研究・研修機構 (2022).『データブック国際労働比較 2022』. 労働政策研究・研修機構.
   https://www.jil.go.jp/kokunai/statistics/databook/2022/index.html
合同会社ユー・エス・ジェイ　ホームページ. https://www.usj.co.jp/company/
ヤンマーホールディングス株式会社　ホームページ. https://www.yanmar.com/jp/
株式会社ゴエンジン　ホームページ. https://www.goenjin.co.jp/

Chapter 3

Hardesty, C. (April 7, 2009). "What is Strategy?" *The Wall Street Journal*.
   http://guides.wsj.com/management/strategy/what-is-strategy/
Kotler, P. (1984). *Marketing Essentials*. Prentice-Hall.（宮澤永光・十合晄・浦郷義郎共訳 (1986).『マーケティング・エッ
   センシャルズ』. 東海大学出版会.）
Mullerbeck, E. (2015). Thorpe, I. (Ed.) "SWOT and PESTEL – Understanding your external and internal context for
   better planning and decision-making." *Learning and Knowledge Exchange. UNICEF — Tools, UNICEF KE Toolbox*.
   https://www.unicef.org/knowledge-exchange/files/SWOT_and_PESTEL_production.pdf
OpenStax (2019). *Principles to Management*. Rice University.
   https://openstax.org/details/books/principles-management
Oxford college of marketing (n.d.). "What is PESTEL analysis?" *Oxford college of marketing website*.
   https://blog.oxfordcollegeofmarketing.com/2016/06/30/pestel-analysis/
San José State University, School of Management (2022). "PESTEL Analysis." *Library resources for you research*. San José
   State University, School of Management Homepage. https://libguides.sjsu.edu/SofManagement
The State of Queensland (2022). "PEST analysis." *Business Queensland*. Queensland Government.
   https://www.business.qld.gov.au/running-business/marketing-sales/tendering/improve-approach/understanding-
   buyer/researching/pest
The University of Sydney (n.d.). "Marketing: PESTLE Analysis." *Library of The University of Sydney website*.
   https://libguides.library.usyd.edu.au/c.php?g=508107&p=5994242
池尾恭一 (2016).『入門・マーケティング戦略』. 有斐閣.

Chapter 4

Barney, J. B. (2002). *Gaining and Sustaining Competitive Advantage*, 2nd ed. Prentice-Hall.（岡田正大訳 (2003).『企業戦
   略論―競争優位の構築と持続（上）』. ダイヤモンド社.）
Mullerbeck, E. (2015). Thorpe, I. (Ed.) "SWOT and PESTEL – Understanding your external and internal context for
   better planning and decision-making." *Learning and Knowledge Exchange. UNICEF — Tools, UNICEF KE Toolbox*.
   https://www.unicef.org/knowledge-exchange/files/SWOT_and_PESTEL_production.pdf
The State of Queensland (2022). "SWOT analysis." *Business Queensland*. Queensland Government.
   https://www.business.qld.gov.au/starting-business/planning/market-customer-research/swot-analysis

北居明・松本雄一・鈴木竜太・上野山達哉・島田善道 (2020).『経営学ファーストステップ』.八千代出版.

榊原清則 (2013).『経営学入門（上）第 2 版』.日本経済新聞出版.

NHK 放送文化研究所 (2021).「国民生活時間調査 2020—生活の変化×メディア利用」.
　　　https://www.nhk.or.jp/bunken/research/yoron/pdf/20210521_1.pdf

Chapter 5

OpenStax (2018). *Introduction to Business.* Rice University.
　　　https://openstax.org/details/books/introduction-business

池尾恭一・青木幸弘・南知惠子・井上哲浩 (2010).『マーケティング』.有斐閣.

北居明・松本雄一・鈴木竜太・上野山達哉・島田善道 (2020).『経営学ファーストステップ』.八千代出版.

榊原清則 (2013).『経営学入門（上）第 2 版』.日本経済新聞出版.

平野光俊・江夏幾多郎 (2018).『人事管理—人と企業，ともに活きるために』.有斐閣.

中小企業庁 (n.d.)「不特定多数の人から資金を調達「クラウドファンディング」」.『ミラサポ plus』.
　　　https://mirasapo-plus.go.jp/hint/16461/

トヨタ自動車株式会社 ホームページ．https://global.toyota/

Chapter 6

Herzberg, F. (1976). *The Managerial Choice: To be Efficient and to be Human.* Dow Jones-Irwin.（北野利信訳 (1978).『能率と人間性—絶望の時代における経営』.東洋経済新報社.）

Herzberg, F., Mausner, B., & Snyderman, B. (1959). *The Motivation to Work.* 2nd ed. John Wiley & Sons.（西川一廉訳 (1966). 『作業動機の心理学』.日本安全衛生協会.）

Maslow, A. H. (1943). A theory of human motivation. *Psychological Review, 50*(4), 370–396.

Maslow, A.H. (1970). *Motivation and personality.* 2nd ed. Harper & Row.（小口忠彦訳 (1987).『改訂新版・人間性の心理学』.産業能率大学出版部.）

McClelland, David C. (1987). *Human Motivation.* Cambridge University Press.（梅津祐良・薗部明史・横山哲夫訳 (2005). 『モチベーション—「達成・パワー・親和・回避」動機の理論と実際』.生産性出版.）

稲葉祐之・井上達彦・鈴木竜太・山下勝 (2010).『キャリアで語る経営組織—個人の論理と組織の論理』.有斐閣アルマ.

金井壽宏 (2005).『リーダーシップ入門』.日本経済新聞出版.

株式会社 andu amet　ホームページ．https://anduamet.com/

フィッシュ・バイオテック株式会社　ホームページ．https://fiotec.jp/

株式会社ゴエンジン　ホームページ．https://www.goenjin.co.jp/

有限会社 re・make（「ゆらぎスタイル」の運営会社）　ホームページ．https://yuragi.co.jp/

Chapter 7

北居明・松本雄一・鈴木竜太・上野山達哉・島田善道 (2020).『経営学ファーストステップ』.八千代出版.

平野光俊・江夏幾多郎 (2018).『人事管理—人と企業，ともに活きるために』.有斐閣.

船越多枝 (2021).『インクルージョン・マネジメント—個と多様性が活きる組織』.白桃書房.

古畑仁一・高橋潔 (2000).「目標管理による人事評価の理論と実際」.『経営行動科学』.*13*(3), 195-205.

NHK（2020 年 1 月 31 日）.「"日本型雇用"の行方は？」.『サクサク経済学 Q & A』.
　　　https://www3.nhk.or.jp/news/special/sakusakukeizai/articles/20200131.html

経済産業省 (n.d.).「人生 100 年時代の社会人基礎力」.『社会人基礎力』.
　　　https://www.meti.go.jp/policy/kisoryoku/index.html

内閣府 (2015).「第 1 部 子供・若者の状況．第 4 章 社会的自立．第 1 節労働」.『平成 27 年版子供・若者白書（全体版）』.
　　　https://www8.cao.go.jp/youth/whitepaper/h27honpen/b1_04_01.html

Chapter 8

Kotler, P. (1984). *Marketing Essentials.* Prentice-Hall.（宮澤永光・十合晄・浦郷義郎共訳 (1986).『マーケティング・エッセンシャルズ』.東海大学出版会.）

Kotler, P. & Armstrong, G. (2012). *Principles of Marketing,* 14th ed. Prentice-Hall.（コトラー，P.・アームストロング，G.・恩藏直人 (2014).『コトラー、アームストロング、恩藏のマーケティング原理』.丸善出版.）

池尾恭一 (2016).『入門・マーケティング戦略』.有斐閣.

池尾恭一・青木幸弘・南知惠子・井上哲浩 (2010).『マーケティング』.有斐閣.

久保田進彦・澁谷覚・須永努 (2013).『はじめてのマーケティング』.有斐閣.

牧田幸裕 (2020).『ケースメソッド MBA 実況中継 01—経営戦略とマーケティング』.ディスカヴァー・トゥエンティワン.

Chapter 9

Kotler, P. (1984). *Marketing Essentials.* Prentice-Hall.（宮澤永光・十合晄・浦郷義郎共訳 (1986).『マーケティング・エッセンシャルズ』. 東海大学出版会.）

Kotler, P. & Armstrong, G. (2012). *Principles of Marketing*, 14th ed. Prentice-Hall.（コトラー, P.・アームストロング, G.・恩藏直人 (2014).『コトラー、アームストロング、恩藏のマーケティング原理』. 丸善出版.）

久保田進彦・澁谷覚・須永努 (2013). 『はじめてのマーケティング』. 有斐閣.

牧田幸裕(2020).『ケースメソッドMBA実況中継01 − 経営戦略とマーケティング』. ディスカヴァー・トゥエンティワン.

読売新聞オンライン (2021年9月7日).「「高たんぱく」商品の市場拡大…健康維持につながる認識、消費者に広がる」. https://www.yomiuri.co.jp/economy/20210907-OYT1T50008/

日本ルナ株式会社 ホームページ. https://www.nipponluna.co.jp/

江崎グリコ株式会社 ホームページ. https://www.glico.com/jp/

江崎グリコ株式会社 "バトンドール" ホームページ. https://www.glico.com/jp/shopservice/batondorshop/

Chapter 10

OpenStax (2018). *Introduction to Business.* Rice University. https://openstax.org/details/books/introduction-business

黒川ひろ・坂下翔也・佐藤栄一郎・佐藤真樹・末信尚史・田口琢巳・田村真平 (n.d.).「法人企業統計調査からみる日本企業の特徴：資料２財務指標の例④売上高営業利益率」. 財務総合政策研究所ホームページ. https://www.mof.go.jp/pri/reference/ssc/japan/japan_all.pdf

山浦久司・廣本敏郎編著 (2003).『ガイダンス企業会計入門—手ほどき・絵ほどき・A to Z 第２版』. 白桃書房.

大津広一・我妻ゆみ (2013).『会計プロフェッショナルの英単語100 − 世界の一流企業はこう語る』. ダイヤモンド社.

中小企業庁 (2005).「Q3.「決算書」って、何ですか？」.『中小企業の会計 31 問 31 答』. https://www.chusho.meti.go.jp/zaimu/kaikei/tools/2008/03.htm

中小企業庁 (2005).「Q4.「貸借対照表」って、何ですか？」.『中小企業の会計 31 問 31 答』. https://www.chusho.meti.go.jp/zaimu/kaikei/tools/2008/04.htm

中小企業庁 (2005).「Q5.「損益計算書」って、何ですか？」.『中小企業の会計 31 問 31 答』. https://www.chusho.meti.go.jp/zaimu/kaikei/tools/2008/06.htm

中小企業庁 (2005).「序章 財務基盤強化のために抑えておきたいツボ」.『上手に使おう！中小企業税制 45 問 45 答』. https://www.chusho.meti.go.jp/zaimu/zeisei/faq45/faq01.html

Chapter 11

Ministry of Internal Affairs and Communications, Japan (2020). *White Paper 2020.* Ministry of Internal Affairs and Communications.
https://www.soumu.go.jp/johotsusintokei/whitepaper/eng/WP2020/2020-index.html
"Chapter 2: Section 1. Issues Facing Japan and ICT as Solutions and Means: 2. Initiatives in regions to solve issues with ICT
"Chapter 2: Section 2. Digitalization Movements Leading Up to 2020: 2. Olympic Legacy.

Ministry of Internal Affairs and Communications, Japan (2021). *White Paper 2021.* Ministry of Internal Affairs and Communications.
https://www.soumu.go.jp/johotsusintokei/whitepaper/eng/WP2021/2021-index.html
"Chapter 1: Section2-2. Digital Transformation Again Attracts Attention."

総務省 (2019).『令和元年版情報通信白書』.
https://www.soumu.go.jp/johotsusintokei/whitepaper/ja/r01/pdf/index.html
「令和元年版　情報通信白書のポイント」
「第１章　ICT とデジタル経済はどのように進化してきたのか」
「第２章　Society 5.0 が真価を発揮するために何が必要か」

総務省 (2020).『令和２年版情報通信白書』.
https://www.soumu.go.jp/johotsusintokei/whitepaper/ja/r02/pdf/index.html
「第２章　5G がもたらす社会全体のデジタル化」
「第３章　5G 時代を支えるデータ流通とセキュリティ」

総務省 (2021).『令和３年版情報通信白書』.
https://www.soumu.go.jp/johotsusintokei/whitepaper/ja/r03/pdf/index.html
「序章　我が国におけるデジタル化の歩み」
「第１章　デジタル化の現状と課題」

オバタカズユキ・鈴木毅 (2019年8月16日)．「「リープフロッグ現象」が導く爆発的発展：20年後のアフリカが「世界地図」を変える？」. Future Questions. Yahoo! JAPAN.
https://fq.yahoo.co.jp/Africa/1.html

アマゾンジャパン合同会社 ホームページ. https://www.amazon.co.jp/

Chapter 12

Ministry of the Environment (2021). "Engaging all stakeholders to address marine plastic waste problem. (PILOT Corporation) — 2. Three transitions: Decarbonized society, circular economy, and decentralized society." *Annual Report of the Environment in Japan, 2021.*
  https://www.env.go.jp/content/900457469.pdf
Ministry of Economy, Trade and Industry (2019). *The Guide for SDG Business Management.*
  https://www.meti.go.jp/english/press/2019/pdf/0531_001a.pdf
International Chamber of Commerce. (July 18, 2017). "Business is stepping up for transformational partnerships."
  https://iccwbo.org/media-wall/news-speeches/business-stepping-transformational-partnerships/
環境省 (2012).『グリーン調達ガイドライン (暫定版) 〜バリューチェーンマネジメントの促進に向けて〜』.
  https://www.env.go.jp/policy/env-disc/com/com_pr-rep/rep-ref06.pdf
経済産業省 (2019).『SDGs 経営／ ESG 投資研究会報告書』.
  https://www.meti.go.jp/press/2019/06/20190628007/20190628007_01.pdf
内閣府 (2020).「2.2. ESG の概要」.『令和 2 年度 障害者差別の解消の推進に関する国内外の取組状況調査報告書』.
  https://www8.cao.go.jp/shougai/suishin/tyosa/r02kokusai/h2_02_01.html
住友化学株式会社　ホームページ. https://www.sumitomo-chem.co.jp/
サラヤ株式会社　ホームページ. https://www.saraya.com/
株式会社パイロットコーポレーション　ホームページ. https://www.pilot.co.jp/company/

・ 上記出典 URL の最終閲覧日は、2022 年 12 月 4 日である。

・ 本書に記載された会社名、企業理念 (それに相当するものを含む)、ロゴ、ブランド名、商品名、個人名は、株式会社三修社を通して記載の許諾を得ている。

・ 企業より提供を受けた写真に関しては、掲載ページに提供元を示している。ご協力頂きました企業に感謝申し上げます。

CLIL 英語で学ぶ経営入門

2023 年 2 月 20 日　第 1 版発行
2023 年 3 月 30 日　第 3 版発行

編集責任——— 笹島　茂（ささじま　しげる）
著　者——— 上野　育子（うえの　いくこ）
　　　　　　船越　多枝（ふなこし　たえ）
　　　　　　Brandon Kramer（ブランドン・クレーマー）
発行者——— 前田俊秀
発行所——— 株式会社　三修社

〒 150-0001
東京都渋谷区神宮前 2-2-22
TEL 03-3405-4511 / FAX 03-3405-4522
振替 00190-9-72758
https://www.sanshusha.co.jp
編集担当　永尾真理
印刷・製本——— 日経印刷株式会社

© 2023 Printed in Japan
ISBN978-4-384-33524-8 C1082

DTP　　　　XYLO
表紙デザイン　山内宏一郎（SAIWAI Design）
イラスト　　　カガワカオリ（p.3, p.13, p.34）